Donald Phillip Verene

Philosophical Self-Knowledge
Two Studies

STUDIES IN HISTORICAL PHILOSOPHY

Editor: Alexander Gungov

Consulting Editor: Donald Phillip Verene

ISSN 2629-0316

1 Dustin Peone
   Memory as Philosophy
   The Theory and Practice of
   Philosophical Recollection
   ISBN 978-3-8382-1336-1

2 Raymond Barfield
   The Poetic Apriori:
   Philosophical Imagination
   in a Meaningful Universe
   ISBN 978-3-8382-1350-7

3 Jennifer Lobo Meeks
   Allegory in Early Greek
   Philosophy
   ISBN 978-3-8382-1425-2

4 Vanessa Freerks
   Baudrillard with Nietzsche
   and Heidegger: Towards a
   Genealogical Analysis
   ISBN 978-3-8382-1474-0

5 Thora Ilin Bayer and
   Donald Phillip Verene
   Philosophical Ideas
   A Historical Study
   ISBN 978-3-8382-1585-3

6 Jeffrey Andrew Barash
   Shadows of Being
   Encounters with Heidegger in
   Political Theory and Historical
   Reflection
   ISBN 978-3-8382-1485-6

7 Donald Phillip Verene
   The Philosophic Spirit
   Its Meaning and Presence
   ISBN 978-3-8382-1781-9

8 Geoffrey Dean
   The Orphic I
   A Philosophical Approach to
   Musical Collaboration
   ISBN 978-3-8382-1629-4

9 Gerasim Petrinski
   The Image of the Demon in
   Byzantium
   Philosophical and
   Mythological Origins
   With a foreword by Prof.
   Georgi Kapriev
   ISBN 978-3-8382-1785-7

10 Donald Phillip Verene
   Philosophical Self-Knowledge
   Two Studies
   ISBN 978-3-8382-1880-9

Donald Phillip Verene

PHILOSOPHICAL SELF-KNOWLEDGE

Two Studies

Bibliografische Information der Deutschen Nationalbibliothek

Die Deutsche Nationalbibliothek verzeichnet diese Publikation in der Deutschen Nationalbibliografie; detaillierte bibliografische Daten sind im Internet über http://dnb.d-nb.de abrufbar.

Bibliographic information published by the Deutsche Nationalbibliothek

Die Deutsche Nationalbibliothek lists this publication in the Deutsche Nationalbibliografie; detailed bibliographic data are available in the Internet at http://dnb.d-nb.de.

ISBN-13: 978-3-8382-1880-9
© *ibidem*-Verlag, Stuttgart 2023
Alle Rechte vorbehalten

Das Werk einschließlich aller seiner Teile ist urheberrechtlich geschützt. Jede Verwertung außerhalb der engen Grenzen des Urheberrechtsgesetzes ist ohne Zustimmung des Verlages unzulässig und strafbar. Dies gilt insbesondere für Vervielfältigungen, Übersetzungen, Mikroverfilmungen und elektronische Speicherformen sowie die Einspeicherung und Verarbeitung in elektronischen Systemen.

All rights reserved. No part of this publication may be reproduced, stored in or introduced into a retrieval system, or transmitted, in any form, or by any means (electronical, mechanical, photocopying, recording or otherwise) without the prior written permission of the publisher. Any person who does any unauthorized act in relation to this publication may be liable to criminal prosecution and civil claims for damages.

Printed in the EU

*La filosofia è quella materia con la quale
o senza la quale si resta tale e quale.*

Philosophy is that subject with which or
without which things remain just the same.

A maxim

Reading works of literature forces on us
an exercise of fidelity and respect, albeit
within a certain freedom of interpretation.

Umberto Eco, *On Literature*

Tutto, tutto, tutto è memoria.
    Everything, everything, everything is memory.

Giuseppe Ungaretti
In a lecture in São Paulo in 1937

Muse [*thea*], daughter of Zeus, start where you will—
sing for our time too.

Homer, *Odyssey*, Book 1

Contents

Preface 9

Introduction: The Idea of Satire and the Rhetoric of Topics 15

Part I. Satire and Self-Knowledge: A Philosophical Consideration

    1. Aristophanes, "The Thinkery" 27

    2. Lucian, "Philosophies for Sale" 31

    3. Desiderius Erasmus, "True Prudence" 37

    4. François Rabelais, "How Panurge Put to a Non-Plus the Englishman Who Argued by Signs" 41

    5. Jonathan Swift, "The Grand Academy of Lagado" 47

    6. Voltaire, "The Best of All Possible Worlds" 53

    7. James Joyce, "by the light of philophosy, (and may she never folsage us!)" 59

Part II. Memory, Topics, and Self-Knowledge: A Philosophical Retrospect

    8. Hesiod, Mnemosyne 67

    9. Plato, The Block of Wax 73

    10. Aristotle, Anamnēsis 79

    11. Giulio Camillo, The Theater 85

    12. Giambattista Vico, Fantasia 91

    13. G. W. F. Hegel, Er-Innerung 97

    14. James Joyce, "mememormee!" 103

Epilogue 109

Notes 113

Index 119

Preface

In Plato's *Phaedrus*, Socrates appears outside Athens, walking with his friend, Phaedrus, along the river Ilisus. They come to a place where, it is said that Orithuia, the daughter of the Athenian king Erechtheus, while playing with Nymphs, was carried away by Boreas, the north wind. Phaedrus asks Socrates if he believes the story to be true. Socrates replies that anyone who would look into the truth or falsity of such matters would "have to be far too ingenious and work too hard—mainly because after that he will have to go on and give a rational account of the form of the Hippocentaurs and then of the Chimera; and a whole flood of Gorgons and Pegasuses and other monsters, in large numbers and absurd forms, will overwhelm him." To engage in such investigation is to pursue questions that, even if answered, make no difference as to how one is to live one's life.

Socrates continues: "But I have no time for such things; and the reason, my friend, is this. I am still unable, as the Delphic inscription orders, to know myself; and it really seems to me pointless to look into other things before I have understood that. This is why I do not concern myself with them. I accept what is generally believed, and, as I was just saying, I look not into them but into my own self: Am I a beast more complicated and savage than Typhon [a multiform beast with a hundred heads, resembling many different animal species], or am I a tamer, simpler animal with a share in a divine and gentle nature?" Socrates then leaves the question of what he is and moves on to the general theme of the dialogue concerning the relation of oratory to philosophy.

The inscription to which Socrates refers is the precept "Know thyself" (*Gnothi seauton*), which appears on the pronaos of the Temple of Apollo at Delphi, greeting all who enter. This precept is the master key to philosophy. It is attributed to the Seven Sages. Thales is thought most likely to be the author of the precept. Thales, the only philosopher among them, is the figure from whom the history of philosophy begins. The other Sages were lawgivers and rulers.

The remarks that follow are organized as a little book, a philosophical novella, addressed to those who may be inclined to pursue self-knowledge. My aim is to invite readers to think through the issues for themselves. My remarks are no more than those at which I have arrived in my own meditations. Philosophy at first began among the early Greeks as a kind of physics, directing thought toward the explanation of natural events, of what is in the heavens and on earth. Socrates gave philosophy a second beginning when, as Cicero says, he brought philosophy down from the heavens and placed it in cities and homes. For Socrates, not nature but human nature is the proper subject of philosophy.

Socrates was often to be found near the entrance of the Athenian agora, the marketplace in the center of the city, engaged in his method of elenchus. To fulfill the purpose of philosophy Socrates sought the answer to a single question: What is it to be a human being, an *anthrōpos*? This question cannot be answered by individual introspection. It can be pursued only through speech with other human beings, because the humanity of a human being exists through interrelationship with other human beings.

Humanity is not individual. It is social. At the basis of society are all those forms of friendship distinctive to human individuals. Also at the basis of society are language and law, poetry and philosophy. These two bases make all else possible. Only human beings pose speculative questions. The life of animals as well as that of gods and divine beings do not involve the formation of speculative questions. Human beings are the only beings that raise the question of the nature of their own being. In pursuing his method of elenchus, Socrates asks questions of those with whom he engages. His questions proceed in the manner of an attorney at law questioning a witness in court. Socrates asks questions, the answers to which he can anticipate. In so doing, Socrates is seeking to learn the answer to a question that motivates all his specific questions, namely: What is it to be human?

When Socrates passes away into death, drinking hemlock on the order of the Athenian court, he leaves his friends with the problem of self-knowledge unresolved. In the Platonic dialogues, when Socrates turns from the elenchus, because his questions have reached a limit, he often relates a story or tale (*mythos*). The tale is only a possible answer. The tale settles the mind so it can seek a new beginning point from which to think about the subject. Socratic scepticism is at the heart of philosophy. The Socratic question for us takes shape in the form of the history of philosophy. This history is the record of how each philosophy is a topic, a *topos*, from which thought finds a new beginning.

In his account of Greek philosophy in his *Lectures on the History of Philosophy*, Hegel says: "The principle of Socrates is that human beings have to discover and learn [*erkennen*] from themselves what their vocation and final goal are, and also what the world's purpose is, what is true in and for itself; they must attain truth by and through themselves." But this truth is not simply subjective. It is a sense of truth that exists in and for itself because "it is objective, meaning by that not outward objectivity but spiritual universality. This is what is true or, in modern terminology, the unity of the subjective and the objective. This is the universal principle of Socrates."

The universal principle of Socrates is that all thought is a dialectical movement between the subjective and objective, between self and world standing to each other as opposites. This opposition can be seen in irony and in satire. Satire takes us out of ourselves and lets us see ourselves as others see us. Socratic irony and Socratic ignorance make room for satire to enter and for us to enter into satire.

Memory, in which all of the topics of thought reside, lets us see ourselves as we see ourselves. Memory, in the sense of recollection, provides us with a self. To have a self is to find oneself alive in time. To find oneself in time is to have an autobiography. We apprehend our existence in terms of past, present, and future—in terms of what we were, what we now are, and what we may be. We realize ourselves as having an internal life that can be reached by memory and formed by the imagination in connection with ingenuity. Who we are in our actuality is a tale only we can tell. This tale is all we have to comprehend ourselves as human beings.

This tale is not simply subjective because it can be told only through the meanings that exist in words. These meanings are achieved and developed objectively in the forms of human culture, in such forms as myth, religion, common sense, art, history, and science. The autobiography of any individual is a particular embodiment of what has already taken place in culture. We, as individual selves, and collectively, as culture, are continually in the position of the Muses—of bringing together what has been, what is, and what is to come. Culture is recollective memory writ large.

To be without recollective memory and the order it brings into our existence is to cease to be a self. In such a state the human spirit wanders without purpose, unable to distinguish with any precision among past, present, and future. The self, thus affected, while awake passes into a state that the normal self experiences only in the world of dreams, a world the order of which we cannot grasp and over which we have no control. In the dream we find ourselves in the midst of conditions that we cannot comprehend. We recover our selfhood once we are out of the moment of the dream and what is dreamed becomes part of memory or disappears from our conscious experience.

To have a self requires the ability to apprehend the world dialectically, to move our thought from one side of an opposition to the other. Memory allows us to pose one side of an opposition to its other in the sense that the past can be posed against the future. In so doing, the self is given a present, a middle from which to assess the nature of the opposition. As the oppositions in the world enter memory they become part of the life of the self. From this grasp of oppositions the poetic sense of life originates. The poetic sense of life allows us to perceive similarity in dissimilars. It gives us the power to form metaphors and the power to form hypotheses.

The world with its oppositions is always an other to the self. We find ourselves in the theater of nature, in which all that is there plays a specific role in what is a whole. Finding ourselves thus, we form a theater of human nature in which all the actions of human beings join together in a drama of our own roles. To attempt not to play a role in this *Theatrum mundi* is to play a role—the role of the outsider—the role of the misanthrope, or that of the hermit, or that of the insider as outsider, the figure who claims to transcend the limits of roles. Memory lets us hold in mind the various roles of human life and provides us with a basis for our own actions and how we may understand them.

The problem for the human self is to keep itself as something that is continually beyond its roles—to be the human being that makes the roles possible. To acquire this standpoint, memory is essential. Recollective memory gives us this ground to be beyond and more than the roles required for life in human society. Who we are is that which we are to ourselves, transcending the roles in which we engage. These roles in which we find ourselves and which enter into our memory are never what we are. But what we are as human beings beyond our roles is the subject of the Socratic question of self-knowledge that unceasingly guides philosophy. The love of wisdom continually causes us to emerge from the narrative of ourselves and face this question. This question, as mentioned above, is asked only by human beings. It is unknown to animals and irrelevant for the immortal gods.

It is commonly thought that at the center of philosophy is the love of wisdom in the sense of the love of reason and that reason is the distinctive faculty of human beings. Reason requires an object to which it is applied. Memory supplies reason with its object. Memory holds in mind that which comes to us through perception, to which we may then apply reason. When reason takes itself as an object, reason takes the shape of logic. Logic is a systematic ordering of what is originally in language and language is the receptacle of all the meanings that can be. Language is the medium of memory and imagination. It is where we can find the first expression of what can be subjected to reason. Reason is an extension of memory, allowing the mind not only to recollect but further, to understand and to speculate on what is recollected. The fact that all words have histories, expressible as etymologies, makes language the original theater of memory. As the theater of memory, language gives us access to the theater of the world and our actions in it.

In the two parts, the two studies, that follow, I have selected some figures from the history of literature and the history of philosophy. My selections are made on the basis of personal preference. I intend the selections to be a miscellany that the reader can approach in terms of the reader's own interest. In regard to satire, I have chosen works that are directed to philosophy, moving from the ancients to the moderns. In regard to memory, I have taken this same direction.

My list in Part I begins from Aristophanes's attack on Socrates and Lucian's satirical commentary on nearly all the ancient Schools of philosophy, moving to the Renaissance satires of Erasmus and Rabelais, to the eighteenth-century portrayals of theories of knowledge and metaphysics of Swift and Voltaire to James Joyce's inclusion of philosophy in his great "joke" of *Finnegans Wake*. My aim in Part II is to sample what philosophy, in some of its history, provides for understanding memory. My list is framed by two poets—by Hesiod and by Joyce. It moves from Hesiod, who introduces the idea of memory, to the two greatest of the ancient Greek philosophers who come to us after Socrates—Plato and Aristotle—to the little-known figure of Renaissance thought, Giulio Camillo, creator of a theater of memory, to Giambattista Vico, as the chief figure of what has been called the "Counter-Enlightenment," to the Idealism of Hegel, author of the *Phenomenology of Spirit*. I then return to Joyce's literary masterpiece, *Finnegans Wake*, in which we enter memory as a great circle of images and words that take thought back upon itself. The two Joyces remind us that ideas of philosophical significance can be found outside the bounds of what are traditionally seen as works of philosophy.

I thank very much my two of the three Graces, Molly Black Verene and Thora Ilin Bayer, for their assistance in preparing the manuscript.

Introduction:
The Idea of Satire and the Rhetoric of Topics

Philosophy is a form of literature, a way of putting thought into words. Leon, tyrant of Phlius, asked Pythagoras what skill, what wisdom (*sophia*) he possessed. Pythagoras replied that he possessed no *sophia*, but that he was a *philosophos*. In so saying, Pythagoras coined a new term, joining *philia* (friendship, friendly love) with *sophia*. Leon asked Pythagoras to say what kind of person is a *philosophos*. Pythagoras compared *philosophoi* to the spectators at the Great Games at Olympia. The spectators came only to see and to comprehend what occurred at the Games. They were unlike those who came to compete or to use the occasion to engage in transactions of buying and selling. Philosophers, for Pythagoras, are spectators occupied with observing the workings of nature. They are lovers of wisdom. Only the gods are wise.

In Plato's *Phaedo*, Socrates redefines the purpose of philosophy. Socrates says: "Those who rightly philosophize are practicing to die [*hoi orthōs philosophountes apothnēskein meletōsi*]" (67e3-4). Socrates transposes the role of the philosopher from spectator of nature to actor of human nature. The philosopher imitates the gods by means of contemplation (*theoria*). The philosopher imitates the god, but is not a god because the philosopher is mortal. Only the gods are immortal. The love of wisdom pursued by those who are philosophers causes them to express their thought in words and defines the way they approach the oppositions that inhere in human existence.

Satire is the master trope of irony expanded into a narrative portraying a state of affairs that is the reverse of what was expected. Satire is a form of ethical thought in that it explores the distinction between *is* and *ought*. It contrasts what theoretical reason tells us ought to be in matters of human conduct with what we can readily see actually is. Satire differs from ethics in that it presents the difference of is and ought by means of a sense of humor that recognizes the presence of folly in all that is human. Satire at its best is comedy done as a form of instruction. It shares with poetry Horace's principles: to instruct, delight, and move. Through satire we see that a state of affairs that meets with our approval, if regarded more closely, may just as well be the opposite. Because of this constant possibility of folly we should not take ourselves seriously. We must discover how to live in this world with folly as a constant companion, always there in our thoughts and actions.

The other master trope that governs the human spirit is metaphor. Aristotle says: "The greatest thing by far is to be a master of metaphor. It is the one thing that cannot be learnt from others; and it is a sign of genius" (*Poetics* 1459a). Metaphor provides thought with its beginnings. Metaphor is a form of ingenuity or wit (Latin, *ingenium*) and is the power to see similarity in dissimilars. Unless we can see such similarity we cannot begin to think. Ingenuity allows us to put the world together through the image. The imagination brings forth from memory what is originally acquired through perception. Once a perception is stored in memory as an image it can be brought forth by the imagination as if it were once again a perception—something vivid and present before the mind. The power of reason allows us to make what is recalled the subject of a question.

Metaphor unifies. Irony dissembles. Each requires the other. If human life is nothing more than a series of satirical scenes, it is a process that signifies nothing. Satire that is more than simple comedy always calls out for thought to seek a new beginning, a new poetry, a new affirmation of the human. Eloquence requires both master tropes—metaphor and irony. Each is in need of the presence of the other. Their interaction gives the self distance from the object.

Satire, *satura,* is the only literary form claimed by the Romans, although there are traces of it in Greek comedy. *Satura* is literally a dish of various ingredients, a medley. Satire as a literary form can combine prose with verse, and personal opinion with public opinion. It is a medley of thoughts with the aim both to entertain and to improve society by exposing faults and frauds in human activity. It shows us that often what we think we are is not what we are. From a philosophical point of view there are two types of satire—one is satire directed to aspects of the human condition generally; another is satire that has direct connection to philosophy that, at least in part, takes philosophy as its subject.

An author of satire, however, need not take philosophy as the object of satire. Philosophy can be employed as the means of satire. An example of this sense of satire is in the second book of Horace's *Satires*, "A Discourse of Plain Living" (influenced by Lucilius), in which the philosophic doctrine of "the mean" is applied to daily living, eating, and drinking (2.2). Aristotle's famous term—*he mesotēs*—in the *Nicomachean Ethics*, regards virtue as a middle between excess and deficiency.

Horace's "The Follies of Humankind" takes up the doctrine of the Stoics, that all except the wise are mad.

Reference to philosophy can also be found in the *Satires* of Juvenal. In satirizing all that can and does go wrong in the world, Juvenal says: "On the other hand, here's a consolation that even an ordinary person can offer—someone who's not read the Cynics, or the doctrines of the Stoics (the same as the Cynics except for their shirts), who's not admired Epicurus, happy with the plants in his tiny garden?" (13.120-24). To cope with the ills of the world, one need not study the theories of the Cynics or Stoics. One can simply follow the example of Epicurus and withdraw to the pleasures of the garden.

Two further examples of this first type are Petronius, *Satyricon* and Cervantes, *The Ingenious Hidalgo Don Quixote de la Mancha*. Petronius flourished in the times of Claudius (41-54 A.D.) and Nero (54-68 A.D.). The *Satyricon* is famous for its description of an extravagant dinner. It also attacks bad taste in literature and the hollow aspects of society. There is a key passage contrasting former ages with the present. "In former ages virtue was still loved for her own sake, the noble arts flourished, and there were the keenest struggles among humankind to prevent anything being long undiscovered which might benefit posterity. . . . But *we* are besotted with wine and whores and cannot rise to understand even the arts that we developed; we slander the past, and learn and teach nothing but vices. Where is dialectic now, or astronomy? Where is the exquisite way of wisdom? Who has ever been to a temple and promised an offering should he attain to eloquence, or drink of the waters of philosophy?" (88). This lack of culture, Petronius says, is due to the love of money taking over all human affairs.

Miguel de Cervantes Saavedra (1574-1616), of Madrid, lived at the time of Shakespeare. Cervantes published *Don Quixote* in two parts, between 1605 and 1615. The work may originally have been intended as a moral fable, as an attack on the ill effects that romances of chivalry had on their readers, but as it expanded during its writing, it became a romance that might be regarded as a forerunner of the modern novel. In the Prologue Cervantes says that his work will not be like other books, that: "are so crammed with maxims from Aristotle, Plato and the whole herd of philosophers that they amaze their readers, who consider the authors to be well-read, erudite and eloquent. . . . There won't be any of this in my book, because I haven't anything to put in the margins or any notes for the end, still less do I know what authors I have followed in my text so as to list them at the beginning, as others do."

Cervantes concludes his Prologue by alerting the reader that his work is about not only the "history of the famous Don Quixote de la Mancha, reputed among all the inhabitants of the Plain of Montiel to have been the chastest lover and the bravest knight ever seen in those parts for many a long year. I have no desire to extol the service I am rendering you in introducing you to such a noble and honourable knight; but I do want your thanks for making you acquainted with the famous Sancho Panza, his squire, in whom, I believe, I give you a compendium of all the squirely fun scattered throughout the whole troop of vain books of chivalry."[1] Epistemologically, Sancho Panza is the figure of sound common sense who sees things mostly as they are.

In Chapter 8 of the first part of the work is the scene in which Don Quixote claims that the thirty or forty windmills he sees on the plain are giants that he must, in the name of chivalry, meet and confront in battle. "For this is a just war, and it is a great service to God to wipe such a wicked breed from the face of the earth." Sancho replies: "Those over there aren't giants, they're windmills, and what look to you like arms are sails—when the wind turns them they make the millstones go round."[2] Don Quixote unsuccessfully attacks the windmills and then goes on his way, still not accepting Sancho's identification of the "giants" as windmills. Philosophically, Cervantes's history of Don Quixote is a tale of appearance and reality, of self-delusion and self-importance, the result of taking oneself seriously versus the "think and see" realism of Sancho Panza. But philosophy is not the subject of Cervantes's satire. Its subject is the folly of the ideal of chivalry as a way of conducting oneself in the world and the pretentiousness of the tales of chivalry that endorse it.

The second type of satire is illustrated by the examples that follow in Part I. These are direct satires of philosophy and philosophical thinking itself. As mentioned above in the Preface, they range from Aristophanes's comedy, *Clouds*, attacking Socrates, and Lucian's cynicism concerning all types of philosophy, to the Renaissance approaches of Erasmus and Rabelais, to the Enlightenment portrayals of Swift and Voltaire, and to Joyce's jokes in *Finnegans Wake*. Although these form a historical sequence, they are not intended to constitute a history of the subject. They are an album to be viewed for whatever it may provide or suggest.

We come away from these satirical perspectives with a sense of the freedom of thought about philosophy. Philosophy is not diminished by these satires. They offer us a way philosophy can be enjoyed. They do not eliminate philosophy. They offer a sense of humor that reminds us that although in fact we are human we are always lacking the ability to know what we are. This disjunct of being that which we are unable to know is the continuing presence of folly in the human, a presence that we continue to experience. Satire keeps philosophy human. It does not cease the human need for the folly connected to the love of wisdom.

The love of wisdom is not only involved with folly. The love of wisdom depends upon the role memory plays in human thought, which is the subject of Part II. Cicero, in *De oratore*, relates the following regarding the famous poet, Simonides of Ceos, who is said to have invented mnemonics. "There is a story that Simonides was dining at the house of a wealthy nobleman named Scopas at Crannon in Thessaly, and chanted a lyric poem which he had composed in honour of his host, in which he followed the custom of the poets by including for decorative purposes a long passage referring to Castor and Pollux; whereupon Scopas with excessive meanness told him he would pay him half the fee agreed on for the poem, and if he liked he might apply for the balance to the sons of Tyndareus [king of Sparta, father of Castor; Pollux is perhaps a son of Zeus; the mother of both is Leda], as they had gone halves in the panegyric.

"The story runs that a little later a message was brought to Simonides to go outside, as two young men were standing at the door who earnestly requested him to come out; so he rose from his seat and went out, and could not see anybody; but in the interval of his absence the roof of the hall where Scopas was giving the banquet fell in, crushing Scopas himself and his relations underneath the ruins and killing them; and when their friends wanted to bury them but were altogether unable to know them apart as they had been completely crushed, the story goes that Simonides was enabled by his recollection of the place in which each of them had been reclining at table to identify them for separate interment; and that this circumstance suggested to him the discovery of the truth that the best aid to clearness of memory consists in orderly arrangement. He inferred that persons desiring to train this faculty must select localities and form mental images of the facts they wish to remember and store these images in the localities, with the result that the arrangement of the localities will preserve the order of the facts, and the images of the facts will designate the facts themselves, and we shall employ the localities and images respectively as a wax writing tablet and the letters written on it" (2.86.352-54).

Quintilian, in *Institutio oratoria*, also relates this story, but with some variation, making it a twice-told tale. "The first person to have made public an Art of Memory is said to have been Simonides of Ceos. The story is well known. He had composed a victory ode of the customary kind for a boxer who had won the crown. The price had been agreed, but part of it was withheld because Simonides, following the common poetical practice, had digressed into an encomium of Castor and Pollux. He was told to ask for the balance of his fee from those whose deeds he had celebrated. And, according to the story they did indeed pay. A great banquet was held to honour the victory and Simonides was invited, but he was called out of the room by a message that two young men on horseback were said to be asking for him urgently. There were no young men to be found, but he realized from what happened next that the gods were grateful to him. For scarcely had he left the building, when the dining hall collapsed on to the heads of the diners, and so crushed them that the relatives who looked for the bodies for burial could not identify their faces or even their limbs by any marks.

"Then, it is said, Simonides, who remembered the order in which they had all been sitting, restored the bodies to their respective families. . . . This exploit of Simonides seems to have led to the observation that memory can be assisted if localities are impressed upon the mind. Everyone will believe this from his own experience. When we return to a certain place after an interval, we not only recognize it but remember what we did there, persons are recalled, and sometimes even unspoken thoughts come back to mind. So, as usual, Art was born of Experience. Students learn from Sites [*loca*] which are as extensive as possible and are marked by a variety of objects, perhaps a large house divided into many separate areas. They carefully fix in their mind everything there which is notable, so that their thoughts can run over all the parts of it without any hesitation or delay" (11.2.11-18).

The balance due to Simonides was paid by the gods directing the twins, Castor and Pollux, to call out Simonides before the collapse of the roof of the banquet hall that killed Scopas and all of his guests. In Quintilian's account they arrive on horseback. In the *Iliad* Homer says: "Castor tamer of horses and the hardy boxer Pollux" (3.237-38). The gods favored Simonides, but from the point of view of Scopas, Simonides violated a business agreement. Simonides was said to be the first poet to charge a fee for his poems and he was known for his greed.

The method of mnemonics discovered by Simonides is that of "artificial" memory—memory that is the result of training in the selection and use of places to organize images to achieve proficiency in *elocutio*—to speak well on a particular subject, to put thought into words. The person wishing to deliver a speech from memory prepares by selecting particular places, perhaps rooms of quite different decorations and furnishings in a house, so as to create a sequence of vivid images. The points to be made in a speech are associated in advance with the rooms and follow the order of the rooms, all held in memory. The speaker moves in memory from image to image. Each reminds the speaker in turn of the point to be expressed. This memory of the places and their sequence provides the speaker with a technique of inner writing from which to speak.

The practice of mnemonics allows us to recall what we wish to say. It leaves us with the question of how we come to acquire what we wish to say, the argument we wish to make. We cannot come to an argument by the principles of what Aristotle calls "analytics." These are the principles by which we can distinguish between correct and incorrect reasoning. Analytics, or what we know as the theory of the syllogism, presupposes that there are deductive arguments already present to be evaluated for their validity or invalidity. To form an argument, to bring it before the mind, we must engage in dialectical rather than deductive reasoning. Dialectical reasoning originates from "topics" (*topoi*), mental places or common places.

Aristotle opens his work, the *Topics*, with the sentence: "The purpose of the present treatise is to discover a method by which we shall be able to reason from generally accepted opinions about any problem set before us and shall ourselves, when sustaining an argument, avoid saying anything self-contradictory." He says further: "Reasoning is a discussion in which, certain things having been laid down, something other than these things necessarily results through them. Reasoning is *demonstration* when it proceeds from premises which are true and primary or of such a kind that we have derived our original knowledge of them through premises which are primary and true. Reasoning is *dialectical* which reasons from generally accepted opinions. Things are true and primary which command belief through themselves and not through anything else; for regarding the first principles of science it is unnecessary to ask any further question as to 'why,' but each principle should of itself command belief. Generally accepted opinions, on the other hand, are those which commend themselves to all or to the majority or to the wise—that is, to all of the wise or to the majority or to the most famous and distinguished of them" (100a-b).

In regard to the categorical syllogism, topics is the art of putting forth the middle term. Once the middle term is found dialectically by comparing views on a subject until a common opinion is found, the major and minor terms of the syllogism can be brought forth and connected to each other by connecting each to the topical middle term. In the categorical syllogism the middle term remains in the premises, making possible the connection through its copula (some form of the verb "to be") of the major and minor terms in the proposition that is the conclusion. Without the middle term there is no syllogism. Once it makes possible the connection of the two terms of the conclusion, the validity or invalidity, the deductive correctness, of the argument can be evaluated by the principles of analytics.

The art of the middle term is an activity of rhetoric through its ability to engage in contentious argument in an attempt to establish what is generally accepted opinion on a given subject. Logic depends on rhetoric to provide the beginnings upon which its arguments are based. Without dialectical reasoning there is no deductive reasoning. The two are inseparable twins; they are the two spheres of reason. Neither can supply what the other supplies.

When the self comes to reason about itself it requires such topics, places from which to begin and from which to draw forth from itself, its treasure-house of memory, what it can think itself to be. The source of self-knowledge is human culture. In the whole of human culture the self is writ large. Culture is the macrocosm of which the individual self is the microcosm. Self-knowledge cannot be reached by engaging in psychological introspection. Self-knowledge can be generated only by education. Education is not training. Training is achieved by direct instruction. Education is dialectical. At the heart of education is the question. Questions are inherently dialectical, especially if they concern some aspect of the human condition. Such questions have no simple answers.

Education gives us access to the topics, the places that culture provides as middle terms from which to reason about the nature of what is human. Education, understood as something beyond receiving instruction, is the approach to wisdom, to a shaping of the soul. Its meaning is present in the Greek word *paideia*. Education in this sense is the bringing together of culture, tradition, literature, and art—forms that directly express the human in relation to what is human. The meaning of *paideia* is embodied in modern consciousness in the German word *Bildung*, in its sense of education as cultivation, the acquisition of not only theoretical knowledge but also of taste, perspective, imagination, and style of thought. From *Bildung* comes *Bildungsroman*, the novel that puts forth the spiritual development of its protagonist.

Education in its true sense is the development of the human spirit. It is a process in which the individual comes to ask the Socratic question of what a human being is. What a human being is stands before the individual in terms of what the human being does in the making of the world of culture. Education is memory. To be educated is to be able to bring to mind what is gained from the past and to have it bear on the present. Memory depends on the medium of language. Reasoning requires words and words bring with them their own pasts. The aim of self-knowledge and of the educated human being is to acquire rational imagination joined with eloquence. Eloquence as the aim of the educated individual is not simply to speak in an elegant style but to put the whole into words. Other than to do no harm, we can wish for little else.

I
Satire and Self-Knowledge
A Philosophical Consideration

1. Aristophanes, "The Thinkery"

Aristophanes's *Clouds* was first produced at the Dionysia of 423. The subject of this comedy is an attack on Socrates, based on three false claims: that Socrates founded a school or *phrontisterion* (a "thinking shop" or "thinkery"); that he taught a doctrine that replaced the gods as the causes of natural phenomena with naturalistic explanations and thus promoted atheism; and, that he was an arch-sophist, training the young in rhetorical skills, without concern for the truth but as a means to overcome adversaries and achieve fame, power, and wealth. *Clouds* did not win the competition, taking only third place, causing Aristophanes to begin a revision of the play for a second production, The revision was never completed, but the part that was revised was put into circulation.

Aristophanes's portrayal of Socrates influenced the popular opinion the Athenians formed of Socrates. When Socrates was brought to trial by Meletus, Lycon, and Anytus in 399, they could presume the negative image of Socrates developed by Aristophanes. In Plato's *Apology* Socrates attributes the charges against him to reflect what is said in Aristophanes's comedy. He says to the jury: "For you too have seen them in Aristophanes's comedy, someone called Socrates swinging around there claiming that he's treading on air and burbling a lot of other nonsense of which I have no understanding great or small" (19c).

The affidavit of the charges against Socrates accord precisely with the claims made of Socrates's activity in *Clouds*. As Diogenes Laertius reports it: "This indictment and affidavit is sworn by Meletus; the son of Meletus of Pitthos, against Socrates, the son of Sophroniscus of Alopece: Socrates is guilty of refusing to recognize the gods recognized by the state, and of introducing other new divinities. He is also guilty of corrupting the youth. The penalty demanded is death" (2.40). In the *Apology*, Socrates puts it this way: "I must read out their affidavit: 'Socrates is guilty and wastes his time seeking what's below the ground and in the heavens, and makes the weaker argument the stronger one and teaches others these same things'" (19b). Socrates is accused of what the philosophers were attempting before him, going back to Thales, namely, a kind of scientific naturalism, and of that in which the Sophists in his own time were engaged, namely, the rhetorical techniques of politics, legal tactics, and business negotiations, for which they charged a fee.

Aristophanes's intention in his comedies was to produce a highly moralistic attack on his subjects. These comedies are satirical but lack the intelligence, finesse, and subtle humor found in works by such great satirists as Erasmus, Rabelais, Voltaire, and Swift. In *Wasps*, Aristophanes includes a speech by the Chorus Leader, deprecating the audiences of his plays. In this speech we find the purpose of these plays stated: "When he [Aristophanes] first began to produce, he says, he didn't attack ordinary people, but in the very spirit of Heracles he came to grips with the greatest monsters. . . . Such a bulwark against evil, such a purifier of the land had you found, when last year you double-crossed him [by not awarding *Clouds* first prize], when he sowed a crop of brand-new ideas that you made fruitless by your failure to understand them clearly. And yet over and over again he swears solemnly by Dionysus that no one ever heard any comic poetry better than that" (1037-47). He says those in his audience have disgraced themselves by not appreciating his genius. Aristophanes's genius is both crude and cruel. Although Aristophanes regards his attacks as full of humor, they are humorless in intent. There is nothing of the value of real folly to be found in his comedies.

In *Clouds*, the Thinkery is presented as a kind of cult, with Socrates as its leader. The play opens with Strepsiades, whose son, Phidippides, spends his time in horse-racing and wagers; he has incurred a great amount of debt against his father's estate. Strepsiades has heard that in the Thinkery pupils can learn how to use language in an unjust way, so as to best their adversaries. He wishes to have his son become a pupil in the Thinkery so as to be able to overcome his creditors and dismiss his debts. When his son refuses to be bothered to acquire this education, Strepsiades enrolls himself. Socrates appears to Strepsiades overhead, suspended in a basket.

Then begins a discourse regarding Clouds, considering the belief that Zeus is the cause of many natural phenomena, including rain. Socrates says: "What do you mean, Zeus? Do stop driveling. Zeus doesn't even exist!" Strepsiades replies: "What are you talking about? Then who makes it rain? Answer me that one, first of all." Socrates says: "These Clouds do, of course! And I'll teach you how, with grand proofs. Now then: where have you ever seen rain without Clouds? Though according to you, Zeus should make rain himself on a clear day, when the Clouds are out of town" (368-70). In this passage Aristophanes has Socrates unequivocally deny the existence of the greatest of the state divinities, Zeus. Zeus is replaced by a wholly naturalistic explanation. If Zeus does not exist, then no gods exist, according to the Socrates of Aristophanes.

Enough has been said about the natural world. Strepsiades is anxious to turn to instruction in the rhetorical tricks that will allow him to acquire practice in unjust argument. With such argument he can overturn his creditors's attempts to collect the debts he owes. Strepsiades says that he does not care to learn any of the stuff Socrates has been discussing. Socrates says: "What *do* you want, then?" Strepsiades replies: "That one, that, that Very Worst Argument!" Socrates says: "But there are other things you must learn before that; say, which of the quadrupeds are strictly speaking masculine." Aristophanes has Socrates professing the prescriptions the Sophists teach regarding grammatically precise usage. This type of pedantry is at the heart of sophistic, intended to impress their pupils.

Strepsiades says: "I certainly know the masculine ones, if I'm not daft: ram, billy goat, bull, dog, fowl." Socrates comments: "Do you see your mistake? You use the same word to refer both to the female fowl [hen] and the male [cock]." Strepsiades then asks Socrates to tell him what is correct. Socrates replies: "'Fowless,' and the other is 'fowl.'" Strepsiades is greatly impressed and says: "Fowless? By Air, that's good" (655-69). The term being discussed as to its gender is *alektruōn*. Strepsiades is so impressed that he later explains this point to his son, as well as informing him that Zeus does not exist (827-51), declaring to Socrates of his son, Phidippides: "He's a born philosopher at heart" (877-79). Strepsiades is thus shown as assisting in teaching Socrates's ideas to the young.

In regard to the charge that Socrates substitutes naturalistic explanations for physical phenomena, denying the presence of gods in nature, Socrates in the *Apology* says that he does not deny the reality of spirits—*daimones*, semi-divine beings that are the offspring of gods and mortals, who act as intermediaries between the gods and mortals. Socrates says: "I do believe in gods, if indeed I do believe in spirits. But if again the spirits are the same kind of offspring of the gods or children of nymphs, or indeed any others they are said to come from: what human being would believe that children of gods exist but not gods?" (27d).

The unstated issue is that Socrates in his arguments in the agora may seem to have suggested that he grasped something about the nature of things that was more than could be seen by the bodily eye. In defining ethical qualities, probably as a reaction to the relativism of the Sophists, Socrates conceives of *eidē* in the form of definitions. In so doing, he does not move completely away from the original meaning of *eidos* as it is in

Homer—as "what can be seen," the "shape of something." But Socrates does not make Plato's claim that the *eidē* exist apart from what can be perceived by the senses (*Tim.* 52a-c). Aristotle says: "Socrates did not make the universals or the definitions exist apart" (*Meta.* 1078b).

In the death scene of the *Phaedo*, after Socrates has drunk the hemlock, he is covered with a blanket. He uncovers his head and says to Crito: "We owe a cock to Asclepius. See to it, and don't forget" (118). These were Socrates's last words. They are usually interpreted to mean that, since Aesclepius is the god of healing, Socrates is saying that death is the cure for the sickness of life. A cock, or rooster, is the least expensive sacrifice that can be made. Socrates uses the same word, *alektruōn*, on which Aristophanes plays in having Socrates begin the instruction of Strepsiades in sophistry. Asclepius is the son of Apollo, and Apollo's father is Zeus. If Zeus does not exist, there is no Asclepius. In this way Socrates shows his belief in Zeus as well as his rejection of sophistry. Socrates, through his skill in irony, has answered Aristophanes in a single sentence, and passed into memory.

2. Lucian, "Philosophies for Sale"

Lucian of Samosata (c. 120-190 A.D.) wrote in the form of satiric dialogue. He was not a philosopher or a moralist, but a rhetorician. His aim was not to reform society. His aim was to amuse. His sale of philosophies is a sale of various types of philosophic life, represented by various philosophers. The sale is organized and directed by Zeus and conducted by Hermes. The buyers are seeking direction for their own careers. Hermes says: "Under the blessing of Heaven, let the buyers now appear at the sales-room. We shall put up for sale philosophies of every type and all manner of creeds; and if anyone is unable to pay cash, he is to name a surety and pay next year" (1). Hermes concludes the sale by saying: "We invite you all here tomorrow, for we intend to put up for sale the careers of laymen, workingmen, and tradesmen" (27). This conclusion suggests that philosophic lives require nothing special. They can be acquired as readily as any other types of lives.

The lives at the sale are those of the Pythagorean, Cynic, Cyrenaic, Democritean, Heraclitean, Academic, Epicurean, Stoic, Peripatetic, and Sceptic. There are ten such lives. Lucian shows us that these ancient philosophies represent more than types of thought. They are embedded in corresponding types of lives. They represent a satirical alternative to the Seven Sages. Note that the Socratic life as such is not included. Plato, not Socrates, is the primary representative of the Academics. Although some of these lives go back to the Pre-Socratics, as a group they are predominantly post-Socratic. There is an allusion to the speech of Alcibiades on Socrates in the *Symposium* (216d-219d), but there is no mention of a life dedicated to the elenchus enacted in the agora. Socrates cannot be considered an Academic because the Platonic Academy was founded after Socrates's death.

The Pythagorean is presented as Pythagoras himself. Hermes says: "The noblest of philosophies for sale, the most distinguished; who'll buy? Who wants to be more than man? Who wants to apprehend the music of the spheres and to be born again?" (2). Pythagoras was said to believe in the reincarnation of souls and to have discovered the numerical ratios determining the principal intervals of the musical scale. He interpreted the world as a whole through numbers, based on the famous Tetraktys that symbolized the perfection of Number and the elements which comprise it. The Buyer asks: What does Pythagoras know best? Hermes replies: "Arithmetic, astronomy, charlatanry, geometry, music and quackery; you see in him a first-class soothsayer" (2). As the Buyer decides to buy Pythagoras, he says: "Come strip, for I want to see you unclothed. Heracles! His thigh is of gold! He seems to be a god and not a mortal, so I shall certainly buy him" (6). Pythagoras was said to have a golden thigh, a sign of his divine status. The Buyer believes that he will be acquiring a place in the brotherhood that Pythagoras has founded.

Hermes turns to the next, the Cynic, Diogenes of Sinope, who appears in a filthy, wretched condition, and carrying a club. The Buyer tells Hermes he does not know to what use he might be put. Hermes says: "If you make him a doorkeeper, you will find him far more trusty than a dog. In fact, he is even called a dog" (7). Cynic is derived from *kyōn* (dog). The Cynics represented a life of virtue, free from the burden of any societal conventions.

Many things are said of Diogenes that are presupposed by Lucian, but not mentioned, such as: that Diogenes slept in a jar, which was in fact a large vessel of the type that was often used as a coffin to bury indigents; that he was observed masturbating in public, and, when chided for such behavior, he patted his stomach and said: "Were this organ so easily satisfied." Once at a feast people kept throwing bones at him, as at a dog, thereupon he urinated on them, in the manner of a dog. He was once captured and sold as a slave, and when the Crier asked what he was good at, he replied: "governing men," and to ask if anyone would like to purchase a master. He was asked why people gave money to those that were lame or blind but not to philosophers, to which he replied that people expect they might become lame or blind but they do not expect to become philosophers. When a definition of man as a "featherless biped" was put forth in the Platonic Academy, Diogenes, it is said, brought a plucked fowl into the lecture rooms, saying "here is Plato's man," causing "with broad nails" to be added to the definition.

Having heard from Diogenes a description of the anti-social life of the Cynic, the Buyer says: "Get out with you! The life you talk of is abominable and inhuman" (11). But he says he will take Diogenes, to use possibly as a boatman or a gardener. Hermes quickly accepts the offer, saying: "We shall be glad to get rid of him because he is annoying and loud-mouthed and insults and abuses everybody without exception" (11).

To move forward from this unpleasant sale, Hermes brings out a Cyrenaic, who represents the view that pleasure is the highest good. The Buyer wishes to question him, but Hermes says that it is not possible for the man to reply, as he is drunk. The Buyer asks who would want to have such a person. Hermes replies that he would be a good companion with whom one could riot about town, and that: "He is a connoisseur in pastries and a highly expert cook: in short, a Professor of Luxury" (12). But the Buyer says: "You had better look about for someone else, among the rich and wealthy people; for I can't afford to buy a jolly life" (12). Hermes concludes they are stuck with keeping this one.

Hermes now brings forth Democritus of Abdera and Heraclitus of Ephesus, to be bid on as a pair. Democritus is known as the laughing philosopher, amused by all human affairs. Heraclitus is said to cry because of a morose personality and because of his view that all things are in constant flux and subject to decline. No one shares their views. They are both left unsold.

To counteract this unpopular pair, Hermes brings forth Academic philosophy. The Academic is Plato, whose school is called Academy because of its location near the site dedicated to the Attic hero Hecademus. The Buyer wants to know Plato's manner of life. Plato replies: "I dwell in a city that I created for myself, using an imported constitution and enacting statutes of my own" (17). The reference is to Plato's *Republic*, which presents an ideal city in speech. Lucian has ignored or perhaps is not aware of Plato's statement in the *Laws* regarding such a state: "It may be that gods or a number of the children of gods inhabit this kind of state; if so the life they live there, observing these rules, is a happy one indeed" (739d-e).

The Buyer says he would like to hear of one of Plato's enactments in his state. Plato replies with one that has become well-known to readers of the *Republic*: "Let me tell you the most important one, the view that I hold about wives; it is that none of them shall belong solely to any one man, but that everyone who so desires may share the rights of the husband" (17). It is not mentioned that this sense of the common family applies only to the Guardian class, not to the *hoi polloi*, who remain with the traditional sense of the household.

Although his purpose is satirical, Lucian makes a point that is quite valuable for the comprehension of Plato's metaphysics. The Buyer asks: "And what is the gist of your wisdom?" (18). Plato replies: "My 'ideas'; I mean the patterns of existing things: for everything that you behold, the earth, with all that is upon it, the sky, the sea, invisible images exist outside the universe." The Buyer asks: "Where do they exist?" Plato says: "Nowhere; for if they were anywhere, they could not be." Plato explains that he sees "two of everything" (18). Plato sees double in the sense that what he sees with the bodily eye is the object as a phenomenon, but he also sees the object with the mind's eye. The mind's eye sees the *idea* or *eidos* of the thing—what makes the thing what it is. Only philosophers have this power of double vision to grasp how a particular perceived object is an image of the form that the mind can see. This "seeing" is the thing as thought, not simply sensed. The Buyer says, rightly: "Then I must buy you for your wisdom and your sharp sight" (18).

Epicurus is now brought forth, and easily sold, because "he is agreeable and fond of good eating" (19). Then Zeus says: "Call another, the one over there with the cropped head, the dismal fellow from the Porch [*Stoa*]" (19). Lucian presents the Stoics as highly argumentative, making layers of distinctions based on their mastery of syllogistic logic, and whose philosophy commands the attention of lawyers, politicians, and men of affairs. Such public figures are expert in maintaining their positions by techniques of reasoning that support their actions. The Buyer finds the doctrines and manner of reasoning to his liking.

Zeus then says to bring out the Peripatetic, that is, Aristotle. Hermes alludes to a passage in the *Nicomachean Ethics*: "That goods are threefold, in the soul, in the body, and in things external" (26; *Nic. Eth.* 1098b). The Buyer declares that Aristotle has "common sense" and offers to buy. Indeed, what we now think of as a commonsense understanding of the nature of things comes in large part from the treatises of Aristotle.

The final figure is brought forth, the Sceptic, represented by Pyrrho of Elis, who would not make any judgments that would go beyond immediate experience. Pyrrhonian sceptics suspended judgments on all questions, including whether or not anything could be known. As a general doctrine, Scepticism claims that for any argument there is a counter-argument. Scepticism thus brings theoretical as well as moral thought to a dead end. Every argument presupposes a context that is not in doubt. The Sceptic can turn to doubt the truth of the context, and in this manner continue to produce doubt in a series in which another step can always be taken in an unending and unproductive movement of thought.

Sceptical doubt in this sense—that of simply pro and con thinking—differs from dialectical thought. Dialectical thought, the form of thought of true philosophy, has scepticism within it as the principle that accounts for its internal movement. Dialectical thought holds that the True is the whole. Thought, by opposing itself, moves toward an ever-greater sense of things. It thus enlarges the context, the narrative, in which argument takes place. It is a mistake to regard Socrates's claim, that he only knows that he does not know, to be a form of scepticism. Socratic method is a form of dialectical thinking, not a form of scepticism comparable to that of Pyrrho or others who developed it, such as Arcesilaus and Carneades.

It is fitting that Lucian concludes with Pyrrho. Lucian's satire is a literary version of Pyrrhonian scepticism. All philosophies have been put up for sale and disposed in various ways. Lucian's cynicism leaves us with nothing. It is unlike the humanistic satire of Rabelais, Erasmus, Voltaire, and Swift, as well as that of Joyce. Lucian's satire presents us with comic derision, not with a sense of folly and the insight into the self and the human world that the acts of folly provide.

3. Desiderius Erasmus, "True Prudence"

Erasmus of Rotterdam (1466?-1536) was inspired in part by Lucian of Samosata. Erasmus borrows from Lucian's various writings the view, held by many figures of the Renaissance, that the world is a stage, a theater in which all are actors playing their various roles. Shakespeare, in *As You Like It*, gives his audience the lines: "All the world's a stage, and all the men and women merely players. They have their exits and their entrances, and one man in his time plays many parts. . . ." (Act 2, scene 7). Erasmus says: "Now what else is the whole life of mortals but a sort of comedy, in which the various actors, disguised by various costumes and masks, walk on and play each one his part, until the manager waves them off the stage?"[3]

Erasmus's famous book, known in English by the title *Praise of Folly*, was titled by Erasmus in Latinized Greek as *Moriae Encomium*. He dedicated his book to his friend Thomas More, on whose name the title is a pun. More kept a fool in his household, whose presence he regarded as valuable. The fool is an agent of honesty, making us aware that what we say or do at any time may not be as wise as we think it to be, and that the reverse may be just as plausible. Folly is worthy of praise for possessing this ability. Folly is not the opposite of self-knowledge; it is a necessary part of it. It causes us always to consider the opposite of what we may have been told to be wisdom, and thus is itself a kind of wisdom. Folly reminds us that there is not a simple division between truth and error. Instead we realize that all that is true is partially error and all error is partially true. As mortals we are always in the middle of this process of what is partial.

Moria (Greek) is the same in meaning as Latin *stultitia*—foolishness, folly, silliness. An encomium is a eulogy or panegyric, one of three types of oration treated in classical theory of rhetoric. The other two are forensic (i.e., judicial) and deliberative. Quintilian, referring to Aristotle and Cicero, says that these three types can be thought to correspond to the three classes of audience: "One meeting for pleasure, one to receive advice and one to judge Causes" (3.4.6). Erasmus's first line is: "However mortal folk may commonly speak of me (for I am not ignorant how ill the name of folly sounds, even to the greatest fools), I am she—the only she, I may say—whose divine influence makes gods and men rejoice."[4] The reader is not only delighted by her presence but also instructed and moved to consider how to judge the world and how thus to act in it.

The key to acting in the theater of the world is to have a grasp of prudence (*phronēsis, prudentia*). Erasmus says: "The wise man runs to books of the ancients and learns from them a merely verbal shrewdness. The fool arrives at true prudence, if I am not deceived, by addressing himself at once to the business and taking his chances."[5] Aristotle says, in the *Nicomachean Ethics*: "Prudence is yoked to the virtue of one's character, and it to prudence, if in fact the principles of prudence are in accord with the moral virtues and what is correct in the moral virtues accords with prudence" (1178a).

Prudence is necessary in order to accomplish all successful human moral action. *Phronimos*, the prudent human being, has the intellectual virtue of prudence. Possessing *phronēsis* permits such a human being to choose the correct action in a situation and to act for the right reason. Aristotle says: "The same person does not admit of being at the same time both prudent and lacking in self-restraint [*enkrateia*]; for it was shown that, as regards his character, a prudent person is at the same time serious as well" (1152a). The fool does not engage in moral arguments pro and con. The fool is not motivated by argument or theory. The fool's talent is to act in terms of a particular situation, taking the chance that what is done is what the situation requires. The fool can act in this way because the fool has insight into both sides of anything. Because of this insight into the doubleness of all things, the fool can immediately take the middle way. Folly permits "going between the horns" of the dilemma.

Erasmus intends to demonstrate that folly is a kind of wisdom, a wisdom that is always in touch with what it means to be human. Erasmus has folly declare: "I emulate those ancients who, to avoid the unpopular name of philosophers, preferred to be called Sophists."[6] Since Socrates, Sophists have been regarded as those who wish to gain acceptance from an audience, whereas philosophers seek to discover the truth. However, the original sense of the Sophist is someone who is wise. The wisdom of satire is what Erasmus seeks in his praise of folly. Folly lets us see through the pretense of any way of thinking that claims to overcome the dialectic of truth and error.

Those who are truly wise are those who can incorporate folly into their thought and actions. But those who insist that their thought transcends any element of what is foolish are messengers of the greatest sense of folly. Erasmus says: "Wherefore, since in fact they are *mōrotatoi*, 'most foolish,' and yet are eager to seem wise men and veritable Thaleses, shall we not with entire justice dub them *mōrosophous*, 'foolosophers'?"[7] To attempt to possess a manner of thought and action that is free from all folly is the greatest folly of all. Those who claim to be without folly are without humor and the happiness that humor can bring into one's life and affairs. Those without humor are unable to see how "foolishness gave rise to cities, by it empires are maintained, along with magistracy, religion, policy, and courts; nor is human life in general anything but a kind of fool's game."[8]

Folly says: "In sum, no society, no union in life, could be either pleasant or lasting without me."[9] There can be no society composed simply of contemplative thinkers. Society requires there to be persons who will take risks, who will attempt things that will take them wherever their passion leads. Erasmus says: "Indeed, we distinguish a wise man from a fool by this, that reason governs the one, and passion the other."[10] Furthermore: "The part of a truly prudent man . . . is (since we are mortal) not to aspire to wisdom beyond his station, and either, along with the rest of the crowd, pretend not to notice anything, or affably and companionably be deceived. But that, they tell us, is folly. Indeed, I shall not deny it; only let them, on their side, allow that it is also to play out the comedy of life."[11]

To be mortal is to know that reason is not everything. To be happy is just to live in the best way one can. This sense of living involves the fact that all is not as it might be. Erasmus says, through the voice of Folly: "And now I seem to hear the philosophers disagreeing with me. But the true unhappiness, they say, is to be engrossed in folly, to err, to be deceived, not to know. Nay, this is to live as a man. Why they call it 'unhappy' I cannot see. It is simply that men are born thus, trained thus, constituted thus; it is the common lot of all. Nothing can be called unhappy if it fulfills its own nature. . . ."[12] The true prudence is to see how to make the best of things in whatever way we can.

In the end, we who are inclined to philosophy may turn to Socrates. Erasmus says: "How ineffective these philosophers are for the work of real life, the one and only Socrates himself, who was judged wisest by (not the wisest) oracle of Apollo, will serve for proof. When he tried to urge something, I know not what, in public, he hastily withdrew to the accompaniment of loud laughter from all quarters. Yet Socrates was not altogether foolish in this one respect, that he repudiated the epithet 'wise,' and gave it over to God; he also cherished the opinion that a wise man should abstain from meddling in the public business of the commonwealth."[13]

Once we acknowledge the overriding presence of folly in all that is human, we may point to Socrates as our guide to thought. Socrates's method of the question that leads to the further question, his grasp of irony, and his profession of ignorance, allow us to be thinking beings in the world.

In his view of Socrates, Erasmus shares a view with his precursor, Sebastian Brant, in *Das Narrenschiff (The Ship of Fools)*, who, in the final compartment of the Ship, says:

> A good, wise man of prudence rare,
> As one can find scarce anywhere
> In all the world, is Socrates—
> Apollo gave him gifts like these—.
> His own judge he, and wisely taught.
> Where he lacks wisdom, fails in aught,
> He gives himself the acid test,
> Heeds not the nobleman's behest
> Nor things the common herd would beg.
> He's oval-shaped, is like an egg,
> That never alien blemish may
> Adhere to him in slippery way.[14]

These concluding lines take the reader back to Brant's Prologue, in which we find, regarding *The Ship of Fools*:

> For fools a mirror shall it be,
> Where each a counterfeit may see.
> His proper value each would know,
> The glass of fools the truth may show.
> Who sees his image on the page
> May learn to deem himself no sage,
> . . . .
> With caution everyone should look
> To see if he's in this my book.[15]

Brant and Erasmus are not the same. Brant is more moralistic; Erasmus is more humanistic, more lighthearted. Yet they share a view of the Socratic unpretentious approach to wisdom. Their attention to folly reminds us of how much in the progress of modernity we have lost this sense of ourselves and the human condition of which folly is a part.

4. François Rabelais, "How Panurge Put to a Non-Plus the Englishman Who Argued by Signs"

François Rabelais (c.1494-c.1553) was a French physician, humanist, and satirist, who published works on archaeology and medicine in Latin, but is most remembered for *Gargantua and Pantagruel*, written in French, which remains unique in French literature, as well as in world literature. Rabelais had command of a great number of French dialects as well as an encyclopedic vocabulary, extending to a dozen contemporary languages. He is a Renaissance figure, who considers gaiety of mind a supreme good. In the chapters here under discussion, Rabelais looks back on the medieval world of Scholastic philosophy.

Pantagruel is the son of Gargantua. They are both giants, who embody all aspects of the human condition. In their adventures they are the intellect, will, and appetites writ large. Pantagruel meets Panurge while walking outside Paris with his entourage of students. Panurge is a young man in a distressed state; misfortune has reduced him to the level of begging. Pantagruel asks him to say his name and tell where he is from. Panurge first answered with a general statement in German. Pantagruel could not understand him, and asked him to speak in another tongue.

Panurge then replied in an imaginary language that was in fact gibberish. He then spoke in Italian, then in Scots, then in Basque, then in another imaginary language, then in Dutch, then in Spanish, then in Danish, then in Hebrew, then in classical Greek, then in another imaginary language that Pantagruel says sounds like what is spoken in Utopia, and then in Latin, the universal language of scholars. Pantagruel asks him if he can speak French. Panurge replies that he can speak French very well, as it is his mother tongue. Panurge is a living pandect—an encyclopedia, a work completely covering all subjects. He is good at anything; there is nothing he cannot do. Pantagruel perceives this in him and immediately adopts him as a friend and disciple. Their adventures together begin. Unlike Pantagruel, Panurge was not a giant but a man of middle height.

After several chapters relating incidents demonstrating Panurge's abilities, including expertise in matters of law, there appears an Englishman who announces that he has come to Paris with the sole purpose of meeting Pantagruel and finding out if Pantagruel's knowledge matches his reputation. He encounters Pantagruel and Panurge as they are in the garden of the Abbey of Saint Denis and "philosophizing after the fashion of the ancient Peripatetics."[16]

The name of the Englishman is Thaumaste, a play on the Greek word for "wondrous" (*thaumasios*). Not only does the fact that Panurge and Pantagruel are philosophizing as Peripatetics, in the manner of Aristotle, but Thaumaste's name recalls Aristotle's famous claim in the *Metaphysics*, that: "It is through wonder [*thauma*] that men now begin and originally began to philosophize" (982b). According to Aristotle, wonder is a response to an *aporia*, a difficulty that occurs because of conflicting arguments. In the *Topics* Aristotle says: "When we are reasoning on both sides of a question and everything appears to have equal weight on either side, we are perplexed which of the two courses we are to adopt" (145b). *Thauma*, then, is not a cosmic feeling about the nature of the universe; it is produced within the process of reasoning. Socrates's claim concerning his own ignorance is caused by the inability of reason to reach a conclusion and provide an answer to the questions he asks.

Thaumaste says to Pantagruel that he has come "solely for the purpose of seeing and conferring with you about certain passages of philosophy, and geometrical divination, and also of cabalistic knowledge, passages of which I am myself unsure and about which I cannot rest content. If you can resolve these difficulties for me, I will be your servant from this day forth, and not only me but all my posterity."[17] Thaumaste, the wonderous, is seeking to resolve various *aporiai*. In an elaborate statement, he says he does not wish to engage in a disputation in a sophisticated manner, arguing simply in terms of for and against. He says: "Nor do I wish to dispute after the fashion of academics, by declamation, or by the use of numbers, as Pythagoras did and as Pico della Mirandola, at Rome, wished to do."[18] Thaumaste's reference is to Pico's proposal to defend nine-hundred *Conclusiones* or theses in the manner of the scholastic disputes of Paris before the Vatican.

Thaumaste says: "I wish to dispute simply by signs, without a word being spoken, for these are matters so intricate and difficult that, as far as I am concerned, mere human speech will not be adequate to deal with them." Pantagruel agrees to these terms and to meet for the disputation the next day, at seven in the morning. He commends Thaumaste on the proposal to dispute "by using signs, without any words, for thus you and I will truly understand one another, free from the sort of hand clapping and applause produced during their discussions by these puerile sophists, whenever one party has the better of the argument."[19]

When someone does not understand something said or there is confusion about something meant, it is possible in some instances to use a gesture to clarify. There are two types of gestures that can be employed and which underpin articulate speech. Gestures can be used to imitate what is meant in the manner of sign languages, such as a movement of the hands to imitate water or wind. In articulate language this sense of imitation can be achieved by onomatopoeia. Gestures can also be used indicatively, to point to an object meant. The act of imitation varies according to what is meant. The act of indicating or pointing is repetitive. The same act is used to direct attention to various objects. In articulate language the act of pointing is replaced by the referential use of words. Words refer to objects. The use of signs in the proposed disputation takes neither of these forms. The disputation will be a version of pantomime, functioning such that one sign confronts another in a self-enclosed set of movements. It will satirize the self-enclosed world of Scholastic speech in which the meaning of words entails the meaning of other words.

Rabelais is satirizing the artificialization of language in philosophy that developed in medieval philosophy from the writings of Anselm of Canterbury (1033-1109), who is often regarded as the father of Scholasticism, to those of Duns Scotus (1266-1308), until challenged by William of Ockham (c.1285-1347), who placed propriety on the side of ordinary speech over the technical side. Scholastic disputation is the opposite of Socratic elenchus, which proceeds from the meanings of words as commonly understood to what these words can mean as expressions of philosophical thought.

In the *Ion* Socrates says he has "nothing else to tell besides the truth after the fashion of the ordinary man" (532c). In the *Gorgias* Socrates is accused of "continual talk of shoemakers and cleaners, cooks and doctors" (491a). In the *Euthyphro* Socrates questions Euthyphro, a religious expert, about the meaning of *hosion* (piety or holiness), going through a progression of possible meanings (5d). In so doing Socrates is attempting to invest ordinary Greek words with philosophical meaning. The Scholastic artificialization of language abandons Latin as in any way once used as a natural language as can be found in comedies such as those of Plautus and Terence. Scholastic Latin creates a terminology of technical meanings that only those schooled in such can understand. Disputations carried on in terms of these meanings are self-enclosed events. The general audience can only pretend to understand what they are hearing.

Prior to the disputation, Pantagruel is up all night, studying works on numbers and signs, on inexpressible things, and on things that cannot be uttered, perusing works by the Venerable Bede, Plotinus, Proclus, Artemidorus, Anaxagoras, Dinarius, Philiston, Hipponax, and many others. Panurge, on realizing that Pantagruel is engaged in such intense preparation, tells him that he should go to bed. Panurge says not to worry, as he will dispute Thaumaste himself. Panurge then spends the night drinking with the servants and playing dice. The next morning, with the audience assembled from all over Paris, Panurge proposes to Thaumaste that he take the place of Pantagruel, while Pantagruel acts as moderator.

Thaumaste agrees, and begins with a sequence of complicated hand signs, to which Panurge replies with his hand signs. Suddenly Thaumaste speaks aloud: "And yet if Mercury—." Panurge immediately tells him to be silent, and the exchange of hand signs continues.[20] Thaumaste's mention of Mercury is perhaps an obscure reference to a story regarding Mercurius, the Latin offshoot of the Greek god Hermes, who is the messenger of Zeus. As Hermes Psychopompos, he was instructed by Zeus, in anger, to convey Lala (chatterer, *laleō*; to talk, chat, prattle, babble) to the underworld. Because of all she had blurted out about Zeus (Jupiter), she was deprived of the power of speech. Panurge has the power to deprive Thaumaste of the power of speech and to convey him back into the world of signs.

The disputation continues with an exchange of ribald bodily signs, including Panurge waving his codpiece about, into which he had placed a large orange. Thaumaste pulls out a dagger, holding it with the point facing down, a sign of surrender, using an object, not a bodily sign. Thaumaste makes several further motions, until: "Panurge put his forefingers on each side of his mouth, pulling back as far as he could and showing all his teeth. His thumbs drew his lower eyelids as far down as they would go, making an exceedingly ugly face, or so it seemed to everyone watching."[21] It is the sign of the clown, the exaggerated smile with drooping eyelids and the masks of comedy and tragedy that are affixed to either side of the stage of a theater. Thaumaste is defeated. Thaumaste, with a tip of his hat, graciously thanked Panurge and said to the audience, in a loud voice: "Gentlemen, now I can truly speak the biblical words: *Et ecce plus quam Solomon hic*, and here is one who is greater than Solomon. You see in front of you an incomparable treasure: and that is Monsieur Pantagruel."[22] Panurge is thanked and Pantagruel is lauded because he is the mentor of Panurge.

Rabelais with his preposterous semiotics has made the disputation a human event. We cannot look at the disputations of Scholastic philosophy in the same way again. We now see that when philosophy is reduced to the exchange of argument and definitions, philosophy becomes simply debate, with one side trying to dominate the other. It is the attachment to critical thinking taken to its unfortunate natural limit. To recover, philosophy must re-enter the world of reason, joined with the imagination. Argument is always a part of philosophical thinking, but when argument absorbs all of philosophical thinking, philosophy becomes dull and lifeless. The tendency to make philosophy about only the formulation of arguments is not confined to medieval Scholasticism, it is always present. The philosopher must learn from the satirists as well as from the poets the extent of language as the medium of thought. It is the metaphor, not the technical term, that always gives philosophy a new starting-point, from which we can begin again with the unanswered question.

5. Jonathan Swift, "The Grand Academy of Lagado"

Jonathan Swift (1667-1745) was born in Dublin and was educated there at Trinity College. In 1726 he published *Gulliver's Travels*, the best known of his large number of works. Swift is among the greatest of satirical writers in English and in world literature generally. Gulliver's travels take him "into several remote nations of the world," one of which is Balnibarbi, an island nation the metropolis of which is called Lagado and which contains the Grand Academy.

Gulliver is engaged in his travels in the early part of the Enlightenment, the showpiece of which was *L'Encyclopédie* of Diderot and d'Alembert, published between 1751 and 1776, in thirty-five volumes. The Enlightenment, the term originally taken from the German *Aufklärung*, is generally identified with the philosophic, scientific, and rational spirit developed in the eighteenth century. Philosophy shifts its attention from the problem of metaphysics, the problem of being, to the problem of knowledge, and from the *esprit de système* to the *esprit systématique*. Swift's satirical attention to the forms, acquisition, status, and promotion of knowledge is ahead of its time.

The problem of knowledge considered as the central problem of modern philosophy has two prominent spokesmen whose works are precursors of the Enlightenment—the English empiricist John Locke (1632-1714) and the French rationalist René Descartes (1596-1650). I have in mind Locke's *An Essay Concerning Human Understanding* (1690) and Descartes's *Discours de la Méthode* (1637). Locke's sensationalistic psychology and epistemology exerted an influence on the *Encyclopédie*. D'Alembert, in his famous *Discours préliminaire*, revealed that the work would go forward in the spirit of Locke's thought. The Enlightenment was committed to a kind of common sense that could be employed by the individual and that could be sharpened by training in logic and "natural philosophy," the term employed for natural science. The Enlightenment stood for reason, nature, and progress.

One thinks here of the fascination of the followers of Diderot and d'Alembert with Jacques de Vaucanson's mechanical figures, including his marvelous mechanical duck that could peck corn, grind it in its internal gears, and defecate—while they watched. Julien Offray de la Mettrie, author of *L'homme machine* (1748), regarded Vaucanson's flute player and duck as demonstrating that it would be possible to make a talking man. He saw in Vaucanson's work the possibility of *"un nouveau Prométhée."* We could transform the material world into our world and make ourselves part of it.

Locke begins his *Essay* with the claim: "It is the *understanding* that sets man above the rest of sensible beings, and gives him all the advantage and dominion which he has over them."[23] Descartes begins his *Discours* with the ironic sentence: "Good sense [*bon sens*] is the best distributed thing in the world: for everyone thinks himself so well endowed with it that even those who are hardest to please in everything else do not usually desire more of it than they possess."[24]

Most philosophers associated with the Enlightenment rejected Descartes as dogmatic because of his attachment to metaphysics. Descartes was regarded as the main representative of the *esprit de système*, involved with a priori reasoning and abstract thinking, not in accord with the commitment of the *philosophes* to empirical inquiry and knowledge. The exception to this view of Descartes is his promotion of method as crucial to the sciences, expressed in the subtitle of his *Discours*, that he intends it *"Pour bien conduire sa raison, & chercher la verité dans les sciences"* (For rightly conducting one's reason and seeking the truth in the sciences).[25] Descartes's formulation of his four-step method for reasoning in the sciences, although rationalistic, modeled on mathematical thinking, not empirical investigation, is what makes him the father of modern philosophy and modern scientific thinking. Descartes intended his method to be demonstrated in three essays, on Optics, Meteorology, and Geometry.

In Swift's report on Gulliver's visit to the Grand Academy of Lagado, both the Lockean and the Cartesian conceptions of knowledge are put in satirical perspective. Gulliver first observes a series of preposterous scientific experiments, such as "extracting Sun-Beams out of Cucumbers, which were to be put into Vials hermetically sealed, and let out to warm the Air in raw inclement Summers." A second experiment "was an Operation to reduce human Excrement to its original Food, by separating the several Parts, removing the Tincture which it receives from the Gall, making the Odour exhale, and scumming off the Saliva." Another experiment involved a "Man born blind" instructing several blind apprentices how to mix colors for painters by distinguishing them by feeling and smelling.

In another experiment Gulliver encountered a researcher "who had found a Device of plowing the Ground with Hogs, to save the Charges of Plows, Cattle, and Labour," using Acorns, Dates, Chestnuts, and other items of which these animals are fond. "Then you drive six Hundred or more of them into the field, where in a few Days they will root up the whole Ground in search of their Food, and make it fit for sowing, at the same time manuring it with their Dung." This experiment resulted in little or no crop. "However, it is not doubted that this Invention may be capable of great Improvement." Gulliver went into another room, where researchers were attempting to replace silkworms in the production of fabric, with spiders making webs, fed by flies imbedded with colors obtained from various gums and oils, although without current success. There is also an experiment by an astronomer with a sundial adjusted to respond to "the annual and diurnal Motions of the Earth and Sun, so as to answer and coincide with all accidental Turning of the Wind."[26]

Gulliver complains of a "small Fit of the Cholick" or indigestion, and is led in to see a great physician who was famous for curing it by means of a bellows. He observes the physician attempting this procedure, and a variation on it, several times on a dog, but: "The Dog died on the Spot, and we left the Doctor endeavouring to recover him by the same Operation."[27] An editorial note states: "The experiments described in this chapter are based on actual experiments undertaken or proposed by Swift's contemporaries."[28] Swift had captured the mentality of modern scientific research. The professors engaged in the experiments are all highly funded and convinced of the idea of overall progress. The failures are only temporary. They are always "working on it."

Gulliver says: "I had hitherto seen only one Side of the Academy, the other being appropriated to the Advancers of speculative Learning." But before proceeding to this other side, he meets "one illustrious Person more, who is called among them *the universal Artist*. He told us, he had been Thirty Years employing his Thoughts for the Improvement of human life. He had two large Rooms full of wonderful Curiosities, and Fifty Men at work." These men are conducting all types of experiments, including making air into a dry, tangible substance, softening marble for pillows and pin-cushions and others that the universal artist was conducting himself, including an attempt "to sow Land with Chaff, wherein he affirmed the true seminal Virtue to be contained," and in another he hoped "to propagate the Breed of naked Sheep all over the Kingdom."[29] There is nothing too grandiose for the scientific concept of knowledge.

On this other side of the Grand Academy Gulliver encounters a Professor in a very large room, surrounded by forty pupils. The Professor and his pupils were engaged in a project for "improving speculative Knowledge by practical and mechanical Operations." Speculative knowledge is what Pierre Bayle, in his *Dictionnaire historique et critique* (1697), conceived of as the Republic of Letters. The Professor in this side of the Academy has found a solution to the long and difficult process required to attain this form of knowledge. He has invented a contrivance to substitute for the usual method of becoming a learned person, that is, through years of study. For "Every one knew how laborious the usual Method is of attaining to Arts and Sciences; whereas by his Contrivance, the most ignorant Person at a reasonable Charge, and with a little bodily Labour, may write Books in Philosophy, Poetry, Politicks, Law, Mathematics and Theology, without the least Assistance from Genius or Study."

The contrivance was twenty-foot square, placed in the middle of the room. Swift includes a diagram of it, which shows a square with eight crank-handles extended on each side, containing 256 small squares of wood (sixteen horizontal and sixteen vertical, intersecting with each other). "These Bits of Wood were covered on every Square with Papers pasted on them; and on these Papers were written all the Words of their Language in their several Moods, Tenses, and Declensions, but without any Order." The pupils turned the handles, changing the configuration of the words. When a part of a sentence appeared it was read out to four pupils who acted as scribes. The pupils worked at this process six hours a day. The Professor showed Gulliver "several Volumes in large Folio already collected, of broken Sentences, which he intended to piece together; and out of those rich materials to give the World a compleat Body of all Arts and Sciences."[30]

Swift has described the first computer, a contrivance whereby all of human knowledge can be coordinated by a single method that anyone can employ with no need for genius or study. Whatever we may wish to know is available on the computer, including translations of any language. The computer is the fulfillment of Descartes's single method of right reasoning. The computer is the Enlightenment conception of the *Encyclopedia*. All knowledge is in one place. As knowledge is produced by scientific research in the first room of the Academy of Lagado, it can be transferred into the contrivance of the second room and combined with all knowledge, as generated at various places and in various languages throughout the world.

In *A Tale of a Tub* (1697-1700), Swift uses the term "computer" in this regard. He says: "Now the Method of growing Wise, Learned, and *Sublime*, having become so regular an Affair, and so established in all its Forms. . . . It is reckoned, that there is not at this present, a sufficient Quantity of new Matter left in Nature, to furnish and adorn any one particular Subject to the Extent of a Volume. This I am told by a very skillful *Computer*, who hath given a full Demonstration of it from Rules of Arithmetick."[31] *Compotus* (*computus*) goes back to the High Middle Ages, conceived as a science of exact chronology reckoned by rational means.

The problem of knowledge is solved by Locke empirically: "*External objects* furnish the mind with the ideas of sensible qualities, which are all those different perceptions they produce in us; and *the mind* furnishes the understanding with ideas of its own operations."[32] As mentioned above, the problem of knowledge is solved by Descartes in his *Discours* by his four-step method of right reasoning: to begin with what is clear and distinct, to divide any difficulties into as many parts as possible, to reason from simplest to complex, and finally, "to make enumerations so complete, and reviews so comprehensive, that I could be sure of leaving nothing out."[33]

The problem that remains for both Locke's and Descartes's conception of the problem of knowledge is how truly to express the truth. The solution to this problem would naturally require application of the principles of rhetoric. But both Locke and Descartes have dismissed the art of rhetoric from their conceptions of knowledge. Locke says, in his discussion of the "Abuse of Words": "If we would speak of things as they are, we must allow that all the art of rhetoric, besides order and clearness; all the artificial and figurative application of words eloquence hath invented, and for nothing else but to insinuate wrong ideas, move the passions, and thereby mislead the judgment; and so indeed are perfect cheats."[34] Descartes says: "Those with the strongest reasoning and the most skill at ordering their thoughts so as to make them clear and intelligible are always the most persuasive, even if they speak only low Breton and have never learned rhetoric."[35]

Following his visit to "the Advancers of speculative Learning" and his observation of the first computer, Gulliver went to the School of Languages, where he was introduced to "a Scheme for entirely abolishing all Words whatsoever." This scheme allowed the most learned and wise to express themselves by "things." This scheme had "only this Inconvenience attending it; that if a Man's Business be very great, and of various Kinds, he must be obliged in Proportion to convey a greater Bundle of *Things* upon his Back, unless he can afford one or two strong Servants to attend him." In order to converse, according to this scheme, a participant would hold up an object. To show that it was understood, the second participant would hold up a matching object. One's knowledge would be equal to the number of things in one's pack.

Gulliver says: "I have often beheld two of these Sages almost sinking under the Weight of their Packs, like Pedlars among us, who when they met in the Streets, would lay down their Loads, open their Sacks, and hold Conversation for an Hour together; then put up their Implements, help each other to resume their Burthens, and take their Leave." This scheme, Gulliver observes, has the advantage of being a universal language: "And thus, Embassadors would be qualified to treat with foreign Princes or Ministers of State, to whose Tongues they were utter Strangers."[36]

In his conception of the grand Academy of Lagado, Swift has shown the reader the extent to which the wisdom of the ancients has been replaced by the problem of knowledge of the moderns.

6. Voltaire, "The Best of All Possible Worlds"

François-Marie Arouet, under the pseudonym Voltaire, published *Candide ou l'Optimisme* in 1759. The origin of the word *"optimisme"* derives from its use by Leibniz in his *Essais de Théodicée* (1710) to present his doctrine that the actual world is the best of all possible worlds. Leibniz reflects this view in his metaphysics of the *Monadology*. He writes: "Now, as in the Ideas of God there is an infinite number of possible universes, and only one of them can be actual, there must be a sufficient reason for the choice of God, which leads Him to decide upon one rather than another.... Thus the actual existence of the best that wisdom makes known to God is due to this, that His goodness makes Him choose it, and His power makes him produce it."[37]

Voltaire's *Candide* is a satire bringing to light the problematic status of Leibniz's claim. "Theodicy" is from Greek *theos* and *dike* (justice). It is a defense of the justice or goodness of God's creation of the world in the face of the phenomenon of evil that is present everywhere. If God is omniscient, omnipotent, and all good, why has God either incorporated or allowed evil in divine creation? God's existence is independent of the world, but God is the first and final cause of all that is actual in the world. In the world are both what is good and what is evil, as anyone can see.

In his *Dictionnaire philosophique portatif* (1764), under the heading *"Bien (Tout est)"*—All is Good, Voltaire says that Leibniz "did humankind the service of explaining that we ought to be entirely satisfied, and that God could do no more for us, that He had necessarily chosen, among all the possibilities, what was undeniably the best one."[38] Voltaire says that Leibniz's friends asked: What will become of original sin? Voltaire says that Leibniz, privately, had no answer, but declared publicly that original sin was a necessary part of this best of all possible worlds.

Speaking for those friends, Voltaire says: "What! to be chased from a place of delights, where we would have lived for ever if an apple had not been eaten! What! produce in wretchedness wretched children who will suffer everything, who will make others suffer everything! What! to undergo every illness, feel every sorrow, die in pain, and for refreshment to be burned in the eternity of centuries! Is this really the best lot that was available? This is not too *good* for us, and how may it be good for God?" Why did God respond to Adam's and Eve's action as original sin by condemning all generations to a punishment for a transgression over which such generations were not and could not be responsible?

Voltaire then says: "Leibniz realized that these questions were unanswerable; so he wrote thick books in which he did not agree with himself."[39] Voltaire concludes this entry by taking his point even further. He says: "This system of *All is good* represents the author of nature only as a powerful and maleficent king, who does not care, so long as he carries out his plan, that it costs four or five hundred thousand men their lives, and that the others drag out their days in want and in tears."[40] This comment would appear to be blasphemous, as it concerns God as doing no more in creating the human world than demonstrating His great power.

Voltaire says: "So far from the notion of the best of possible worlds being consoling, it drives to despair the philosophers who embrace it. The problem of good and evil remains an inexplicable chaos for those who seek in good faith. It is an intellectual exercise for those who argue: they are convicts who play with their chains. As for the unthinking mass, it rather resembles fish who have been moved from a river to a reservoir. They do not suspect that they are there to be eaten in lent; nor do we know anything by our own resources about the cause of our destiny."[41] We do not know why God allows human affairs to be such that evil enters into them. To claim that things are for the best overall is no consolation for those who are subjected to suffering and adversity.

In Chapter 5 of *Candide*, Candide and his old philosophy tutor, Dr. Pangloss, find themselves aboard a ship along with other passengers, including Jacques the Anabaptist. The vessel is tossed by a storm. The sails are torn, masts break, and the ship is taking on water. A sailor is jolted overboard and Jacques attempts to go to his assistance but is himself thrown overboard. Candide "tries to jump in after him; Pangloss the philosopher prevents him, arguing that Lisbon harbour was built expressly so that this Anabapist should one day drown in it. While he was offering *a priori* proofs of this, the vessel split and everyone perished, with the exception of Pangloss, Candide and the same brute of a sailor who had drowned their virtuous Anabaptist."[42]

The name, Pangloss, is formed from the combination of the Greek words *pan* and *glōssa*, meaning "all tongue," "all talk." Pangloss is one who glosses over everything. Voltaire says those "who speak in order to say nothing" engage in *panglossie*. By contrast, Rabelais's Panurge is "all work," as when he takes over the task of debating Thaumaste. *Candide*, in French, is "innocent, ingenuous, sincere, candid," connected to the Latin *candidus*, "shining white, glittering white," and when used of character it connotes "honest, straightforward."

Having survived the shipwreck, Candide and Pangloss proceed to Lisbon on foot. They arrive just as the Lisbon earthquake occurs. The Lisbon earthquake, in fact, occurred on the morning of the first of November, 1755, killing as many as, by one estimate, 60,000 people. In a letter of November 24th, Voltaire wrote of the event: "This is indeed a cruel piece of natural philosophy! We shall find it difficult to explain how the laws of motion can produce such fearful disasters *in the best of all possible worlds*—when a hundred thousand ants, our neighbors, are crushed to death in seconds in one of our ant-heaps, half of them undoubtedly dying in inexpressible agonies, beneath debris from which it was impossible to extricate them. . . . What a game of chance is human life!"[43] Voltaire wrote a lengthy poem, "The Lisbon Earthquake or An Inquiry into the Maxim, 'Whatever Is, Is Right,'" in which he says that the miseries and horrors that plague humanity: "Prove that philosophy is false and vain." On December 16th, in another letter, Voltaire wrote: "Like you, I pity the Portuguese; but men make even more evil for themselves on their little molehill than nature makes for them."[44]

In the text of *Candide*, on the day following the earthquake, Candide and Pangloss are having a meager meal with some survivors. "Pangloss consoled them, assuring everyone that things could not be otherwise: 'This is all for the best,' he said, 'For if there is a volcano beneath Lisbon, then it cannot be anywhere else; for it is impossible for things to be elsewhere than where they are. For all is well.'" Voltaire then relates how Pangloss is hanged as part of an *auto-da-fe*, "it having been decided by the University of Coïmbra [a city northeast of Lisbon] that the spectacle of a few individuals being ceremonially roasted over a slow fire was the infallible secret recipe for preventing the earth from quaking."[45] Although it is unusual to include a hanging at such an event, it obviously was meant to be. In addition to the hanging of Pangloss, Candide is flogged.

The second word in Voltaire's title is "optimism." Leibniz gave the name "*optimisme*" to his doctrine that this was in fact the best of all possible worlds, in 1737, two years before the earthquake. The reader is not told if Pangloss considers his own fate as another example of what should occur in the best of all possible worlds. But we might expect Pangloss to declare it to be so. In fact, just before the conclusion of the book we learn that Candide and Pangloss are suddenly reunited.

Now reunited, Pangloss relates to Candide that the rope was wet and improperly affixed, so he survived the hanging. He was bought as a corpse by a surgeon, who began dissecting him only to discover that he was alive. Pangloss was sewn back together by a Portuguese barber. Pangloss later entered a mosque, and because of his (respectful) attention to a young female devotee, and because he was discovered to be a Christian, he was arrested and sentenced to be chained to row in a galley. He was released only when ransomed by Candide. Thus reunited, Candide asks Pangloss: "'While you were being hanged, and dissected, and beaten, and made to row in a galley, did you continue to believe that all was for the best?'—'I hold firmly to my original views,' replied Pangloss, 'I am a philosopher after all: it would not do for me to recant, given that Leibniz is incapable of error, and that pre-established harmony is moreover the finest thing in the world—not to speak of the *plenum* and the *materia subtilis*.'"[46]

There are two problems with claiming that this world is the best—that everything happens for the best. Its advocates must explain not only why human beings are such that they persistently commit evil acts upon each other, but further, why, independently of any human cause, human beings are made to suffer from disease and to suffer such natural disasters as the Lisbon earthquake.

To the first, it could be argued that human beings are endowed by God as Creator with free will, and thus there is no necessity that they should become criminals and prey on other human beings, and further argued that overall good does prevail in the world. The question remains, however, as to why God, who made human beings in his own image, did not transfer to human beings this divine goodness. The doctrine of original sin, first developed by St. Augustine, attempts to account for why human beings are as they are. But why did God even allow the Fall as part of original human existence?

To the second question, the doctrine of original sin does not apply. Human beings are made to suffer through natural causes over which they have no control. Human beings cannot decide not to be subject to disease or not to be overtaken by natural disasters. Human beings simply find themselves alive in this world. God is the cause of the world and acts in terms of complete goodness. Why, then, is human life so perilous?

Voltaire's view is that there are no answers to be found to such questions. His solution appears in the last words of his book: "But we must cultivate our garden."[47] We are to turn then, in the end, to Epicurus, whose Garden allows us to retreat from the clamor of society. The Garden of Epicurus is as close as we can come to the Garden of Eden. This Garden is a refuge, a measured optimism within society, and there is no guarantee that it will last, but it is all that we have.

7. James Joyce, "by the light of philophosy, (and may she never folsage us!)"

Joyce is the author of *Dubliners* (1914), *A Portrait of the Artist as a Young Man* (1916), *Ulysses* (1922), and *Finnegans Wake* (1939). These works are the result of Joyce as a literary portraitist. *Dubliners* is a series of portraits of the populace of Dublin in the early 1900s. *A Portrait of the Artist as a Young Man* is a self-portrait. *Ulysses* is a portrait of the ancient hero's return to Ithaca, done in the sequence of one day in the life of Leopold Bloom as he moves about Dublin. *Finnegans Wake* is the portrait of Everybody, represented by the modern family man, Humphrey Chimpden Earwicker, H.C. Earwicker, H.C.E., "Here Comes Everybody." "An imposing everybody he always indeed looked, constantly the same as and equal to himself and magnificently well worthy of any and all such universalisation" (032.18-21).[48]

    Finnegans Wake takes its title from the Irish "Ballad of Tim Finnegan." Tim Finnegan was a hod carrier, who took a drop of whiskey every morning to help him through his day. But one day his tippling was too much, and he fell from the ladder and broke his skull. "So they carried him home, his corpse to wake." At the wake, a gallon of whiskey, the "water of life," was spilled on Tim, causing him to revive and jump from his bed, saying, "Bad luck to your sowls. D'ye think I'm dead?" He was awake. The ballad ends with: "Isn't it all the truth I've told ye, Lots of fun at Finnegan's wake?"

    In 1936, Joyce told the Danish writer, Tom Kristensen, who asked Joyce for help in understanding *Work in Progress*, that was to become *Finnegans Wake*: "Now they're bombing Spain [the Spanish civil war]. Isn't it better to make a great joke instead, as I have done?"[49] To a drinking companion, Joyce once rephrased "*In vino veritas*" to "*In risu veritas*."[50] Joyce insisted the book was a joke. He told Jacques Mercanton, the Swiss critic: "I am nothing but an Irish clown, a great joker at the universe."[51] *Finnegans Wake* is not a satire, but it moves through moments of satiric humor, offset by moments of poetic insight. The reader is presented with a coincidence of opposites, moreover, a series of "cocoincidences" (597.01) in which everything is doubled, and in so doing, "Every talk has his stay" (597.19).

    In the dream world of Joyce's "lingerous longerous book of the dark" (251.24), his book of "nightjoys" (357.18), sixty-five philosophers attend the wake.[52] They range from Plato: "P.t.l.o.a.t.o." (286.03), that is, "Plates to lick one and turn over" (286.18); to Aristotle: "aboove his subject probably in Harrrystotalies" (110.17); to Augustine, the Bishop of Hippo: "the ruah of Ecclectiastes of Hippo outpuffs the writress of Havvah-ban-Annah" (038.29-30); to Thomas Aquinas: "his tumescinqinance" (a reference to his corpulence) (240.08); to Nicholas of Cusa: "the learned ignorants of the Cusanus philosophism" (a reference to his book, *De Docta Ignorantia*) (163.16-17); to Francis Bacon: "with a second course eyer and becon" (406.15); to Descartes: "you make me a reborn of the cards. . . . cog it out, here goes a sum" (304.27-31); to Kant: "tantoo pooveroo quant" (416.13) and Hegel: "hegelstomes" (416.33); to Vico: "Our wholemole millwheeling vicociclometer" (614.27), the device on which all of *Finnegans Wake* is based.

In addition to the list of great philosophers in *Finnegans Wake* there is a list of great poets: Homer: "*the humour of a hummer*" (341.10), and Dante Alighieri: "the divine comic Denti Alligator" (440.06) and the combination of Dante, Goethe, and Shakespeare: "I always think in a wordsworth's of that primed favourite continental poet, Daunty, Gouty, and Shopkeeper" (539.05-6). The presence of such philosophers, intermixed with the presence of such poets, provides us with a basis to resolve the problem that Plato leaves unresolved at the end of the *Republic*, that is, the quarrel between philosophy and poetry. Poetry provides us with images of both good and bad conduct, without supplying us with the means to approve of one over the other. Because of its lack of judgment, poetry must be sent away from the ideal city. Yet Socrates says to Glaucon: "Aren't you, too, my friend, charmed by it [*poiēsis*], especially when you contemplate it through Homer?" Glaucon replies, "Very much so" (607c-d).

Socrates says that poetry and poets had to be banned from the city because "The argument [*logos*] determined us." But, Socrates says: "Let us further say to it, lest it convict us for a certain harshness and rusticity, that there is an old quarrel between philosophy and poetry" (607b). It is then said that poetry should be readmitted to the city if poetry's protectors or the poets themselves would present an apology (*apologia*, defense) on its behalf. But knowing of no such speech, either in meter or by argument, the Platonic Socrates leaves us with the resolution of the ancient quarrel outstanding. It is the one problem that every philosophy must solve. Poetry and philosophy have in common that they each exist through words. The philosopher requires the poet in order to learn the extent of words.

Joyce says: "hoping against hope all the while that, by the light of philophosy, (and may she never folsage us!) things will begin to clear up a bit one way or another within the next quarrel of an hour" (119.04-6). Joyce puts the Greek word for light in "philophosy"—*phōs*, the contraction of *phaos*. In the *De anima*, Aristotle says: "As sight is the most highly developed sense, the name *phantasia* has been formed from *phaos* (light) because it is not possible to see without light" (429a). The *philia* in philosophy is the love of the light or clarity that resides in wisdom. May such love of wisdom never "folsage us"—forsake us. In the *Ion*, poetry is described as a kind of madness. Joyce's line suggests that philosophy may have its own madness. There is a play on *filofol*, that suggests a "fine madness" or "*fine folie*," *fine* (Italian), implying a final or ultimate kind of madness for rational clarity. May philosophy never "folsage us"—"*saige-fol*" ("wise crazy"), never leave us without the light. The philosopher would do well to listen to the music in the words of Joyce's joke.

Jorge Luis Borges says: "I have thought that the word 'thunder' might mean not only the sound but the god. . . . When I speak of night, I am inevitably—and happily for us, I think—reminded of the last sentence of the first book in *Finnegans Wake*, wherein Joyce speaks of 'the rivering waters of, hitherandthithering waters of. Night!' This is an extreme example of an elaborate style. We feel that such a line could have been written only after centuries of literature. We feel that the line is an invention, a poem—a very complex web, as Stevenson would have had it. And yet I suspect there was a moment when the word 'night' was quite as impressive, was quite as strange, was quite as awe-striking as this beautiful winding sentence: 'rivering waters of, hitherandthithering waters of. Night!'"[53]

Samuel Beckett says: "Mr. Joyce has desophisticated language. And it is worth while remarking that no language is so sophisticated as English. It is abstracted to death. Take the word 'doubt': it gives us hardly any sensuous suggestion of hesitancy, of the necessity for choice, of static irresolution. Whereas the German 'Zweifel' does, and, in lesser degree, the Italian 'dubitare'. Mr. Joyce recognizes how inadequate 'doubt' is to express a state of extreme uncertainty, and replaces it by 'in twosome twiminds' [188.14]. . . . Here is the savage economy of hieroglyphics. Here words are not the polite contortions of 20th century printer's ink. They are alive. They elbow their way on to the page, and glow and blaze and fade and disappear."[54]

Joyce realizes that the etymologies of words hold in them all that is in human memory and all that can be acted out in the world. Joyce's aim, in *Finnegans Wake*, is through the power of imagination to take the reader back to the original speech, before the Tower of Babel. In the ten thunderwords, the longest words in the English language, with the first one occurring on the book's first page, the thunderwords prepare us to hear the original speech of humanity as we go through the book. We listen as thunder for the first time comes across Joyce's page: "bababadalgharaghtakamminarronnkonnbronntonnerronntuonnthunntrovarrhounawnskawntoohoohoordenenthurnuk!" (003.03).

To take us back to this original form of speech, Joyce employs the joke. The joke is the most human of all speech acts. The joke is taken to its greatest limit through the trope of irony. Irony is pursued, by Joyce, in the form of the pun. A joke, like a fable, reveals who we are as human beings. "Joke" is most immediately from Latin *jocus*, "jest," "joke," "game," and is akin to Old Saxon and Old High German *gehan*, "to say," "speak," and is related to Middle Welsh *leith*, "language," that can be taken back to Sanskrit *yācati*, "he implores" with the basic meaning of speaking. To joke is to speak, spoke. Joke is associated with Finnegan. "Finnegan" is "end again": *fine*, Italian "end" with the *n* doubled. "Mark Time's Finist Joke"—Mark Tim Finnegan's Joke; Time's Final (Finest) Joke—death (455.29).

Joyce must take us back in memory so that we do not forget the original meanings of words. It is here that philosophy must begin its love of wisdom. The philosopher must go to school with the poets and the poets must look toward the philosophers to see the poetic meanings completed as the esoteric truths of reason. To do so we will need to have "two thinks at a time" (583.07). We find ourselves before ourselves. We face the problem of self-knowledge. Whatever we are, it is to be found in Joyce's great circle of human experience. Joyce has left nothing out.

What is the subject of Joyce's great joke? And why did Joyce call his book, his masterpiece, *Finnegans Wake*? The joke's on us. We are all Finnegans at our own wake. As collective humanity we cannot awake from history. As individual human beings we cannot awake from it either, and furthermore as individual humans we cannot awake from our own mortality. We all must "Mark Time's Finist Joke." Finnegan was not quite dead at his wake but, like all of us, he will at some time be so.

In the last lines of *A Portrait of the Artist as a Young Man*, Stephen Dedalus, who is Joyce, and whose name brings together the Judeo-Christian and the Greco-Roman—the biblical Stephen, the first Christian martyr, and the mythical figure of the ancient artificer *Daidalos*—says: "Mother is putting my new secondhand clothes in order. She prays now, she says, that I may learn in my own life and away from home and friends what the heart is and what it feels. Amen. So be it. Welcome, O life! I go to encounter for the millionth time the reality of experience and to forge in the smithy of my soul the uncreated conscience of my race." Then Stephen adds his own prayer: "Old father, old artificer, stand me now and ever in good stead."[55]

Joyce is about to fly from the labyrinth of Dublin, although he knows not where. It is, however, to Italy where he will search for the smithy of his soul. Daedalus with his wax wings flies from the labyrinth of the palace at Knossos to land in Sicily or Italy. We find ourselves in a world not of our control or comprehension. It is like a dream. We have no control over our dreams. They occur or they do not. And, when they do we have no say in what occurs in them. In our awake world we find ourselves in language, in a world of words, the meanings of which we have not made. But we discover, with Joyce, that we can recombine words in the smithy of our soul and move them about in the conscience of the human race.

Through words we are awake at our own wake, our own life. We can be motivated by the joke. We realize the truth that we can have "Lots of fun" as we are all in one way or another at Finnegan's wake. Our consolation is that there is a providentiality to all events that surround us. This sense that all that happens is what happens is the response to Stephen's request as he begins his flight. Things go on no matter what. We realize, like Finnegan, that we are now at least alive. Once we realize it is all a joke, it becomes our joke and we can say with Finnegan: "Bad luck to your sowls. D'ye think I'm dead?"

II
Memory, Topics, and Self-Knowledge
A Philosophical Retrospect

8. Hesiod, Mnemosyne

Hesiod lived during the eighth century B.C. He was born in Ascra, a small village of Boeotia. He was raised as a shepherd without any training by human teachers. He suddenly found himself able to produce poetry, an ability he attributes to his encounter with the Muses, and he went on to be successful in poetic competitions. The meaning of Hesiod's name is unclear, but it may have an implicit etymology of *Hēsi-odos*, "he who sends forth song." Hesiod is the companion figure with Homer, marking the beginning of Greek culture. These are the two figures joined together throughout Plato's dialogues. Hesiod's works are *Theogony* and *Works and Days*. He is called the "father of Greek didactic poetry."

Hesiod begins the *Theogony* by introducing the Muses to the world. He says: "Let us begin to sing from the Heliconian Muses, who possess the great and holy mountain of Helicon and dance on their soft feet around the violet-dark fountain and the altar of Cronus's mighty son [Zeus]. . . . One time, they taught Hesiod beautiful song while he was pasturing lambs under holy Helicon. And this speech the goddesses spoke first of all to me, the Olympian Muses, the daughters of aegis-holding Zeus: 'Field-dwelling shepherds, ignoble disgraces, mere bellies: we know how to say many false things similar to genuine ones, but we know, when we wish, how to proclaim true things.' So spoke great Zeus's ready-speaking daughters, and they plucked a staff, a branch of luxuriant laurel, a marvel, and gave it to me; and they breathed a divine voice into me, so that I might glorify what will be and what was before, and they commanded me to sing of the race of the blessed ones who always are, but always to sing of themselves first and last" (1-34).

The Muses are divine beings who sing and dance together in a harmonious fashion. The Muses move freely among the other immortals because of the beauty of their presence. When the Muses appear before Hesiod he is no more than a counterpart to the sheep of which he is shepherd. He is a human being, but exists alongside the sheep, eating and sleeping and wandering the earth with them. He is a mere belly. But the Muses invest Hesiod with the divine power of poetry, signified by their gift of the laurel. Its foliage was used by the ancient Greeks to crown victors in the Pythian games. The power of poetry comes only from the gods. Homer begins both his poems with an incantation to the Muses. Even Lucretius, who turns away from the gods, professes in his poem his love of the Muses as responsible for the charm of poetry (*De rerum natura* 1.921-950).

The false songs of the Muses that they can sing similar to genuine ones are not deliberate lies. They are paralogisms. Poets are by nature inclined to state fabrications. They put us in contact with what is fabulous. To do this they can freely commit false inference, what in logic is called *fallacia consequentis*. Aristotle recognized this aspect of aesthetics in the *Poetics*. He says: "Just because we know the truth of the consequent, we are in our own minds led on to the erroneous inference of the truth of the antecedent" (1460a). In *On Sophistical Refutations*, Aristotle says: "The refutation connected with the consequent is due to the idea that consequence is convertible. For whenever, if A is, B necessarily is, people also fancy that, if B is, A necessarily is" (167b). Logic requires that only the antecedent can determine the truth of the consequent: if A implies B, and A is true, only then is B true. This principle of logic, known as *modus ponens*, guides rational deductive thought, but it need not be followed in poetic thought. The imagination can show us its own truth, that reason does not know.

Hesiod says: "Mnemosyne (Memory) bore the Muses on Pieria, mingling in love with the father, Cronus's son—Mnemosyne, the protectress of the hills of Eleuther—as forgetfulness of evils and relief from anxieties. For the counsellor Zeus slept with her for nine nights, apart from the immortals, going up into the sacred bed; and when a year had passed, and the seasons had revolved as the months waned, and many days had been completed, she bore nine maidens—like-minded ones, who in their breasts care for song and have a spirit that knows no sorrow—not far from snowy Olympus's highest peak" (*Th.* 53-63). The Muses represent the arts of humanity, which, like the Muses themselves, are products of memory. The Muses are the offspring of divine memory. The arts are governed by the Muses and are the forms of human memory. The divine element in human beings is represented by the Muses. The Muses oppose evils and provide relief from anxieties, "and the voice they send forth from their mouths as they sing is lovely, and they glorify the ordinances and the cherished usages of all the immortals, sending forth their lovely voice" (65-67).

Poetry in song and dance is the first form of memory in the world of immortal beings, and it is shared with the world of human beings. Each Muse represents a version of the poetic in human experience. They are: "Clio (Glorifying) and Euterpe (Well Delighting) and Thalia

(Blooming) and Melpomene (Singing) and Terpsichore (Delighting in Dance) and Erato (Lovely) and Polymnia (Many Hymning) and Ourania (Heavenly), and Calliope (Beautiful Voiced)—she is the greatest of them all, for she attends upon venerated kings too. Whomever among Zeus-nourished kings the daughters of great Zeus honor and behold when he is born, they pour sweet dew upon his tongue, and his words flow soothingly from his mouth" (76-83). As the Muses become figures in Greek and Roman literature and beyond, they assume further and more specific identities, but they always take us back to their identity with their mother, Mnemosyne.

Solace is the gift of the Muses, the gift of memory. It is with our memories that we live, and deeply rooted in memory is the poetic sense of life. Hesiod says: "Such is the holy gift of the Muses to human beings. For it is from the Muses and far-shooting Apollo that human beings are poets upon the earth and lyre-players, but it is from Zeus that they are kings; and that person is blessed, whomever the Muses love, for the speech flows sweet from that person's mouth. Even if someone who has unhappiness in his newly anguished spirit is parched in his heart with grieving, yet when a poet, servant of the Muses, sings of the glorious deeds of people of old and the blessed gods who possess Olympus, he forgets his sorrows at once and does not remember his anguish at all; for quickly the gifts of the goddesses have turned it aside" (93-103).

That the Muses tell of what was, is, and is to come relieves the anguish of human existence, for the greatest source of anguish is the lack of knowledge of the future. The Muses show that the poet is also a seer. They show that a knowledge of the past allows for a grasp of the present and prepares us for what is to come in the future. For whatever will come in the future, the mind is prepared by the memory of what has happened in the past. The past was once the future that is now absorbed in the present. It is always from the memory of the past, preserved in the power of the Muses, that we are provided with a basis to face the future. To know what can be known is the essence of self-knowledge. Poetry is the primary assertion of the self as present in the world. We make ourselves what we are through what we store in memory and what we do with ourselves.

Hesiod takes up this sense of the self in *Works and Days*. He begins by invoking the Muses, saying: "Muses, from Pieria, glorifying in songs, come here, tell in hymns of your father Zeus, through whom mortal men are unframed and framed alike, and named and unnamed, by the will of great Zeus. For easily he strengthens, and easily he crushes the strong, easily he diminishes the conspicuous and increases the inconspicuous, and easily he straightens the crooked and withers the manly—high-thundering Zeus, who dwells in the loftiest mansions. Give ear to me, watching and listening, and straighten the verdicts with justice yourself; as for me, I will proclaim truths to Perses" (1-10). Poetry directed by the Muses will let us act with the will of Zeus and will let us express the principles of the human world. Poetry is a form of practical wisdom. By guiding poetry the Muses not only refresh our spirit, they inspire us to proper actions.

Hesiod says: "Upon the earth there are two Strifes. One of these a man would praise once he got to know it, but the other is blameworthy; and they have thoroughly opposed spirits. For the one fosters evil war and conflict—cruel one, no mortal loves that one, but it is by necessity that they honor oppressive Strife, by the plans of the immortals. But the other one gloomy Night bore first; and Cronus's high-throned son, who dwells in the aether, set it in the roots of the earth, and it is much better for men. It rouses even the helpless man to work. For a man who is not working but who looks at some other man, a rich one who is hastening to plow and plant and set his house in order, he envies him, one neighbor envying his neighbor who is hastening towards wealth: and this Strife is good for mortals. And potter is angry with potter, and builder with builder, and beggar begrudges beggar, and poet poet" (11-26).

As mortals we find ourselves beset by two kinds of Strife. One is the existence of evil in the world. We can do nothing to eliminate this Strife. It is part of the human condition itself. The other kind of Strife is generated by the differences between the circumstances of one individual versus another. The solution for overcoming this Strife is work. There is continual competition among human beings. Human beings do not live simply by instinct. They can alter the condition of their existence through their efforts. Work is the central fact of human life. Hesiod intends *Works and Days* as a poem that teaches us about the nature of work and thus about ourselves. The didactic nature of his poem sets Hesiod off from Homer. Homer does not present the actions of ordinary people. He speaks of heroes, of Achilles, of his courage and rage, and of Odysseus, the man of twists and turns.

Hesiod concludes his *Works and Days* by saying what the days he has described offer—the ways in which human beings can improve their lives. He says: "These days are a great boon for those on the earth. But the others are random, doomless, they bring nothing. One man praises one kind of day, another another; but few are the ones who know. . . . Happy and blessed is he who knows all these things and does his work without giving offence to the immortals, distinguishing the birds and avoiding trespasses" (822-28). The birds are often guides to the weather and the seasons. What Hesiod describes are days filled with things worth doing. The things worth doing are simple, honest tasks of life that are adjusted to nature. They represent a peaceful existence lived in accord with others and with the processes of nature.

Hesiod, in his two poems, shows us a life wherein our human spirit is nourished by memory, by the way we can access memory through the arts conveyed to us by the Muses. The arts calm the anxieties of human life. They bring peace to our emotions. Hesiod shows us further how we can act in the world in a peaceful and productive manner, how we can be ourselves and not harm others. Hesiod advocates an ethic of decorum that is available to all human beings who are wise enough to grasp his straightforward teaching.

9. Plato, The Block of Wax

Goethe says: "Plato relates himself to the world as a blessed spirit, whom it pleases sometimes to stay for a while in the world; he is not so much concerned to come to know the world, because he already presupposes it, as to communicate to it in a friendly way what he brings along with him and what it needs. He penetrates into the depths more in order to fill them with his being than in order to investigate them. He moves longingly to the heights in order to become again a part of his origin. He expresses a declaration of an eternal Whole, Good, True, Beautiful; he strives to stimulate the summons to these in each breast. What he himself claims regarding each instance of worldly knowledge melts away, indeed it can only vaporize in his method, in his discourse."[56]

In that part of the Platonic corpus designated as *Definitions* there is the following: "*mnēmē*, memory: disposition of the soul which guards over the truth which resides in it" (*Def.* 414a). These definitions are probably a small number of definitions of philosophical terms that were coined and discussed in Plato's Academy. They were of terms used as topics in dialectical discussions within the Academy. This definition is interesting because it asserts that memory is that by which the soul retains truth. We may say that memory is fallible but we can also say that it is that by which we hold on to truth. If we do not remember what has been established as true in the past, what is true disappears, and we must continually rediscover what is true. Memory is the storehouse of truth. It is our only such storehouse.

In the *Cratylus* Plato says: "As for the Muses and music and poetry in general, they seem to have derived their name from their eager desire [*mōsthai*] to investigate and do philosophy" (406a). In the story of the cicadas in the *Phaedrus*, the cicadas and their song are declared to be a gift of the Muses. Socrates says: "Everyone who loves the Muses should have heard of this. The story goes that the cicadas used to be human beings who lived before the birth of the Muses. When the Muses were born and song was created for the first time, some of the people of that time were so overwhelmed with the pleasure of singing that they forgot to eat or drink; so they died without even realizing it. It is from them that the race of cicadas came into being, and, as a gift from the Muses, they have no need of nourishment once they are born. Instead, they immediately burst into song, without food or drink, until it is time for them to die."

Socrates continues: "After they die, they go to the Muses and tell each one of them which mortals have honored her. To Terpsichore they report those who have honored her by their devotion to the dance and thus make them dearer to her. To Erato, they report those who honored her by dedicating themselves to the affairs of love, and so too with the other Muses, according to the activity that honors each. And to Calliope, the oldest among them, and Urania, the next after her, who preside over the heavens and all discourse, human and divine, and sing with the sweetest voice, they report those who honor their special kind of music by leading a philosophical life" (259b-d).

As Hesiod says in his list of the Muses, Calliope is "Beautiful Voiced" and "the greatest of them all." The philosophical life requires divine power of speech to express the ideas that reside in the mind, the divine part of the human psyche. The source of this divine power resides in the heavens, the place of the immortals represented by Urania (*Th.* 75-82). Calliope and Urania are the daughters of Memory who are the most closely connected to the production of philosophy. Socrates says to Crito in the *Phaedo*: "For you know well, my dear Crito, that to express oneself badly is not only faulty as far as the language goes, but does some harm to the soul" (116a).

In the *Theaetetus*, Socrates asks Theaetetus: "Is it possible to learn something you didn't know before?" Theaetetus agrees that this is possible and furthermore that it is possible to keep adding to what is already learned. Socrates says: "Now I want you to suppose, for the sake of the argument, that we have in our souls a block of wax, larger in one person, smaller in another, and of purer wax in one case, more impure in another, in some persons rather hard, in others rather soft, while in some it is of the proper consistency." Socrates here suggests the distinction that in the human world there are those who know (proper consistency of the wax), those who can come to know—the refined (soft wax), and those who do not know, the *hoi polloi* (hard wax).

Socrates continues: "We may look upon it, then, as a gift of Memory, the mother of the Muses. We make impressions upon this of everything we wish to remember among the things we have seen or heard or thought of ourselves; we hold the wax under our perceptions and thoughts and take a stamp from them, in the way in which we take the imprints of signet rings. Whatever is impressed upon the wax we remember and know so long as the image remains in the wax; whatever is obliterated or cannot be impressed, we forget and do not know" (191c-e).

Without memory of perceptions and thoughts nothing can be learned and without learning nothing can be known. The wax tablet of memory contains what we are as human beings. The essence of what we are is what is recorded and preserved on the tablet of humanity and on the tablet of each individual. It contains the education of humanity and the education of each individual.

Socrates never attempts to answer directly the question of who he is as a human being. It is the question he urges everyone to ask of themselves. He considers this urging of each of the citizens of Athens to ask this question, and to pursue its answer above all other concerns, to be his chief contribution to the city. When he is found guilty at his trial, Socrates, in accordance with Athenian law, proposes a penalty he thinks appropriate.

Socrates says: "What is suitable for a poor benefactor who needs leisure to exhort you? Nothing is more suitable than for such a person to be fed in the Prytaneum, much more suitable for such a person than for any one of you who has won a victory at Olympia with a pair or a team of horses. The Olympian victor makes you think yourself happy; I make you be happy. Besides, he does not need food, but I do. So if I make a just assessment of what I deserve, I assess it as this: free meals in the Prytaneum" (*Ap.* 36d-37a). Socrates's ironic proposal is not accepted.

His statement that: "I make you be happy" concerns the term *eudaimonia*. In its literal sense, this is the possession of a good daimon, a good indwelling spirit, a good genius. This daimon that potentially exists in every human being is that to which Socrates's elenchus is addressed. By means of his questions, Socrates intends to arouse this spirit in those human beings who will engage with him. Socrates himself possesses this good daimon but he does not know how or why. It is a gift of the gods and the key to his wisdom.

Socrates might consider bringing forth who he is by attention to the theory of memory advanced in the *Theaetetus*, that all that he is, is recorded in his memory. He might answer his question by an act of recollection that would constitute his autobiography. This autobiography would not need to be written by Socrates, for he wrote nothing. But it might have been written by Plato, from what he could have heard from Socrates, had Socrates spoken of himself and related how he came to be the figure engaged time after time in his elenchus in the agora. How did Socrates become who he is?

Considered from one perspective, the facts of Socrates's life are similar to those that might be attributed to anyone of his *deme* in Athens. He was born of ordinary parents. His mother, Phaenarete, was a midwife and his father, Sophroniscus, was perhaps a stonemason. Socrates served with distinction in military campaigns as a fully armed hoplite. He was plain-living, married, with children. He was devoted to Athens and respected its customs and civic religion. As Diogenes Laertius says: "He was a man of great independence and dignity of character" (*Lives* 2.24). As Xenophon says: "None ever knew him to offend against piety and religion in deed or word" (*Mem.* 1.1.10).

From a second perspective, Socrates is a unique individual. He practiced no profession. As Xenophon describes his day: "Socrates lived ever in the open; for early in the morning he went to the public promenades and training-grounds; in the forenoon he was seen in the agora; and the rest of the day he passed just where most people were to be met: he was generally talking, and anyone might listen" (*Mem.* 1.1.10). One of those people, according to Diogenes Laertius, was Plato. When Plato "was about to compete for the prize with a tragedy, he listened to Socrates in front of the theatre of Dionysus, and then consigned his poems to the flames. . . . From that time onward, having reached his twentieth year (so it is said), he was the pupil of Socrates" (*Lives* 3.5-6).

Socrates is an extraordinary presence in Athens. No one else is like him. The Greeks saw particular persons as instances of various types of human beings. Socrates appears as the great exception to this sense of things. Socrates emerges as an individual who fits into no human type. He is not a politician, a poet, an orator, an artisan, a tradesman, an athlete, or a philosopher, in the sense of the early figures such as Thales or Pythagoras, who were devoted to investigations of the natural world. Socrates appears as a unique individual in the speech of Alcibiades at the end of the *Symposium*. Pierre Hadot says: "It is in Alcibiades's speech in praise of Socrates that the representation of the Individual appears, perhaps for the first time in history. . . . Socrates is impossible to classify; he cannot be compared with any other man. At most, he could be compared with Silenoi or Satyrs. He is *atopos*, meaning strange, extravagant, absurd, unclassifiable, disturbing. In the *Theaetetus*, Socrates says of himself: 'I am utterly disturbing [*atopos*], and I create only perplexity [*aporia*].'"[57]

Socrates introduces the question into philosophy, and shows what it can do in regard to the problem of self-knowledge. The question is inherently dialectical because it is always uncertain what the answer is to the Socratic question. Dialectic is always disturbing because it does not allow for certainty. What may be determined through dialectic is itself always subject to dialectic, to further pursuit of the question. The turning point in Socrates's career came when his friend and admirer, Chaerephon, asked the Delphic oracle if anyone was wiser than Socrates. The Pythian replied that no one was wiser than Socrates. Socrates asked himself the question: "Whatever does the god mean?" After much examination and questioning of others, Socrates says that his wisdom was "that I do not think I know what I do not know" (*Ap.* 21d).

Socrates, however, concludes that he may possess human wisdom: "What kind of wisdom? Human wisdom, perhaps. It may be that I really possess this" (*Ap.* 20d). Wisdom is to have a knowledge of things human and divine and acquaintance with the causes of each. Socrates does not claim to have a knowledge of divine things. The use of the question applies only to the pursuit of human knowledge. Divine knowledge can be sought only by other means. Socrates's concern is to know what human nature is. The answer cannot be found by solitary introspection. It requires discourse with other human beings because to be human is to involve oneself with other human beings.

Although Socrates never tells us how he became Socrates, one incident stands out. It is Socrates's comment on Anaxagoras in the *Phaedo*. Socrates says that one day he heard someone reading from a book of Anaxagoras, "and saying that it is Mind [*nous*] that directs and is the cause of everything" (97c). He says he believed he had found a teacher who would show him that the cause of things is Mind. But he found that Anaxagoras gave only physical causes for all things, including the sun and moon and the other heavenly bodies. Socrates says that then: "This wonderful hope was dashed as I went on reading and saw that the man made no use of Mind, nor gave it any responsibility for the management of things, but mentioned as causes air and ether and water and many other strange things" (98b-c). Socrates says if such were the case then he would be nothing more than the bones and sinews of which his body consists.

Socrates's recollection of this incident makes us wish that he would have gone into his memory more extensively. Then we might have gained the sense of self-knowledge that motivates his elenchus. We can see that Socrates has a grasp of who he is as a human being, more than anyone else he questions, and more than ourselves. But Socrates has no autobiographical account of himself, of what is stored in his memory that shaped him into the figure Plato presents. Who Socrates is remains just beyond our grasp. Socrates's attraction to the universal may have prevented him from giving a speech of himself as particular.

In Plato's dialogues Socrates is recollected in the theater of Greek culture and imagination. The reader of Plato's dialogues soon learns that the figure of Socrates often speaks for Plato, especially in what are traditionally thought of as Plato's later dialogues. Plato began his career as a poet but also as a writer of work for the theater. In writing his dialogues Plato creates, not a series of plays for performance on the stage, but a theater for the mind, a theater of *nous* in which we experience the power of the Socratic question. In the years Plato knew Socrates, he must have listened countless times to Socrates engaging in his method of elenchus. Plato's dialogues are his artful constructions that present us with the enduring presence of Socrates. The dialogues prompt us to engage in self-recollection, because the questions Socrates asks of the players of the roles in Plato's theater become our questions. These questions commit us to philosophy. To attempt to answer them we must re-think what we can recollect of ourselves. We must somehow establish our own agora. That is the position in which we are left by the Platonic Socrates.

10. Aristotle, Anamnēsis

Goethe says: "Aristotle stands to the world as a man, an architect. He is only here once and must here make and create. He inquires about the earth, but not further than to find a ground. From there to a middle point, the earth is for him not a matter of concern. He draws a huge circumference for his building, procures materials from all sides, arranges them, piles them up, and thus climbs, in regular form, pyramid fashion to the top."[58]

Among Aristotle's short treatises on various functions of human life, known as *Parva Naturalia*, is "On Memory and Recollection." Aristotle is concerned to distinguish between memory (*mnēmē*) as the simple act of remembering and recollection (*anamnēsis*) as an act by which human beings think themselves in a particular way in time. He says that it is impossible to remember the future or to remember the present. Perception occurs in the present, "for it is neither the future nor the past that we cognize by perception, but only the present" (449b). All that is in memory was at one time in perception in the present.

Imagination (*phantasia*) is part of memory. Imagination provides memory with the mental images that are the subjects of acts of remembering. Aristotle says: "It is impossible even to think without a mental picture" (449b). The imagination forms and preserves what we acquire in perception. We require mental images not only to complete acts of sense-perception but also to record perceptions in memory. Aristotle says: "Memory, even of the objects of thought, implies a mental picture. . . . It is obvious, then, that memory belongs to that part of the soul to which imagination belongs; all things which are imaginable are essentially objects of memory, and those which necessarily involve imagination are objects of memory only incidentally" (450a).

Recollection is a particular process of memory. Memory in the sense simply of remembering occurs when time has elapsed. We can remember anything in any order, at any time. But recollection is to place our mental images that reside in memory into a deliberate sequence. Aristotle says: "Thus when anyone wishes to recall anything, this will be the method; we will try to find a starting-point for an impulse which will lead to the one we seek. This is why acts of recollection are achieved soonest and most successfully when they start from the beginning of a series; for just as the objects are related to each other in an order of succession, so are the impulses" (452a).

In order to recollect, it is useful to start from a middle point. Aristotle says: "For instance, suppose one were thinking of a series, which may be represented by the letters ABCDEFGH; if one does not recall what is wanted at A, yet one does at E; for from that point it is possible to travel in either direction, that is either towards D or towards F. If one does not want one of those, one will remember by passing on to F, if one wants G or H. If not, one passes on to D. Success is always achieved in this way" (452a). It is important to locate a fruitful starting-point to accomplish the full act of recollection.

Recollection, like memory in general, occurs in time, but unlike memory regarded as simple remembering, recollection is an ordering of time in terms of a particular sequence. Aristotle says: "Recollecting differs from remembering not merely in the matter of time, but also because, while many other animals share in memory, one may say that none of the known animals can recollect except human beings. This is because recollecting is, as it were, a kind of inference; for when we recollect we infer that we have seen or heard or experienced something of the sort before, and the process is a kind of search" (453a). The ability to recollect requires the faculty of deliberation, and deliberation is a kind of inference. In recollecting one is seeking to have one thing remembered to be the ground of another that stands to it as a consequent.

How may we regard self-knowledge as connected to recollection? In recollection the self is engaged in an act that only the self can perform. The self can recollect what is not itself, but in so doing what is not itself becomes part of itself. In recollection the self is seeking its autobiography. What the individual self is, is what it can recall and order of itself. This order depends upon finding a *topos*, a center from which what is already in memory can be grasped as having a starting-point and a finish. Aristotle underscores the importance of the middle. It is the middle term from which we construct a syllogism and it is the middle (*to meson*) or the mean (*mesotēs*) by which we arrive at the virtues that stand between two vices—one of excess and the other of constriction—that guide our moral choice and action.

Recollection is implicitly a narrative. When expressed in words it is a narrative in which the self forms itself. This narrative requires imagination. Aristotle says in the *De anima* that: "Imagination is different from both perception and thought; imagination always implies perception, and is itself implied by judgment. But clearly imagination and judgment are different modes of thought. For the former is an affectation which lies in our power whenever we choose (for it is possible to call up mental pictures, as those do who employ images in arranging their ideas under a mnemonic system), but it is not in our power to form opinions as we will; for we must either hold a false opinion or a true one" (427b).

Aristotle says that in imagination we are like spectators looking at a picture. But imagination is different from sensation. He says: "All sensations are true, but most imaginations are false" (428a). Sensations are true because they are simply what they are. The truth of sensations is immediate. Sensations are not inferences. In acts of imagination we are in the position of the Muses—of singing both true and false songs. Judgment applied to the mental images we form from the imagination introduces the power to evaluate these images as to their truth or falsity through rational discourse.

If we employ imagination as a means to see who we truly are, imagination is recollection. Imagination, as the power to bring forth mental images as if they were perceptions, joined with judgment to order one image as the basis of another in a dialectical sequence, provides us with a way of thinking of ourselves. We are what we can know ourselves to have been. What we are at present, and will become, is based on what we have been in our past that we access through recollection.

Aristotle gives a number of definitions of a human being (*anthrōpos*). Of a human being, "it is appropriate to say 'A human being is an animal'" (*Topics* 102a). A human being is "by nature a civilized animal . . . an animal capable of receiving knowledge" (*Topics* 128b and 132a). "For as a human being is the only animal that stands erect, a human being is also the only one that looks directly in front; and the only one whose voice is emitted in that direction" (*Parts of Animals* 662b). A human being is "the only animal that laughs" (*Parts of Animals* 673a). "It is clear also that the soul is the primary substance and the body is matter, and human being or animal is the compound of both taken universally" (*Meta.* 1037a).

Regarding a human being as an ethical being, Aristotle says: "For just as for a flute-player, a sculptor, or any artist, and, in general for all things that have a function or activity, the good and the 'well' is thought to reside in the function, so would it seem to be for a human being, if a human being has a function" (*Nic. Eth.* 1097b). Only human beings experience happiness. Aristotle says: "The activity of the god, because it is superior in blessedness, would be contemplative. And so in the case of the human activities, the one that is most akin to this would be most characterized by happiness [*eudaimonia*]. A sign of this is also that the rest of the animals do not share in happiness, because they are completely deprived of such an activity. For to the gods, life as a whole is blessed; but to human beings, it is blessed to the extent that something resembling such an activity is available. But none of the other animals are happy, since they in no way share in contemplation [*theōria, theōrein*]" (*Nic. Eth.* 1178b).

Regarding language, Aristotle says in the *Politics*: "A human being is the only animal who has the gift of speech.... And it is a characteristic of a human being that a human being alone has any sense of good and evil, of just and unjust, and the like, and the association of living beings who have this sense makes a family and a state" (1253a). In the *Poetics* Aristotle says: "Imitation [*mimēsis*] is natural to a human being from childhood, one of a human being's advantages over the lower animals is this, that a human being is the most imitative creature in the world, and learns at first by imitation. And it is also natural for all human beings to delight in works of imitation" (1448b).

In Aristotle's early dialogue, the *Protrepticus*, we find: "Since nature is endowed with reason, no matter what form nature assumes, nature does nothing haphazardly, but always and everywhere acts for an end. Rejecting chance, nature is concerned about the end more than are the arts, especially since the arts are but imitations of nature. Since a human being is by nature composed of soul and body, and since the soul is better than the body, and since that which is inferior is always the servant of that which is superior, the body must exist for the sake of the soul."[59]

Aristotle goes on to say that the soul has a rational part and an irrational part and that the irrational part exists for the sake of the rational part. The rational part is the mind and the activity of the mind is the production of thoughts. Thinking is the seeing of the objects of thought, just as sight is the power to see objects of sight. The mind, Aristotle holds, is the best part of the soul. Human beings are rational animals who at their best direct the mind toward thoughts that are considered for their own sake and are not pursued for the sake of something else. The pinnacle of thought, then, as mentioned above, is thought as contemplation. Contemplation is the art of looking upon something with the sole purpose of comprehending what it is. This comprehension is sought as an end in itself, having no further purpose of doing or making something as a result of its comprehension.

This list of the properties that distinguish human beings from other animate beings, which runs throughout many of Aristotle's treatises, is one form of self-knowledge—that which can be gained by means of definition *per genus et differentiam*. But once these definitions are formulated there is little more to say beyond amplifying them with further details. The second sense of self-knowledge is what can be formulated through recollection, as described above. This sense of self-knowledge is the formulation of a narrative generated from acts of recollection. This narrative is a product of memory joined with reason. The narrative must make rational sense of what is drawn forth from the past as held in memory. What we are is what we can recollect of ourselves and bring to bear on the present. How we form the past in the present determines on what we can rely in regard to the future. It is a process that allows us to accept time, to accept our own mortality.

11. Giulio Camillo, The Theater

Giulio Camillo Delminio (c.1480-1544), was one of the most famous figures of the sixteenth century, known to his contemporaries as "the Divine Camillo." He was later forgotten except for some brief mention in the eighteenth century. Who was this unique Renaissance figure? Lina Bolzoni, in *Il teatro della memoria: Studi su Giulio Camillo*, gives this description: "Fat and stammering, speaking like someone possessed and thus reducing to silence sceptical men of letters and refined courtiers; of an obscure family, with little disposable money, fabled of wealthy Croatian origins, of a splendid erudition that waits only to be recouped, and on this basis asks for a loan from an unfortunate admirer who, in the hope of rejuvenation, drank one of his miraculous discoveries, a 'potable gold' that reduced the admirer to the end of his life.

"He moves with a great natural ease, from distant Friuli to the intellectual circles of Venice and Padua, to Bologna with the daring '*notomisti*' and heretical groups, to Rome with the 'Ciceronians' (and then within the conclave that elects Pope Farnese), to the villas of the patricians of Genoa, to the splendid French court of Francis I, the Geneva of Calvin, to the Milan of D'Avalos, where he dies as a result of excessive amorous exercise with two women, he who transported himself from Venice to France and back again to Italy. Man of letters and philosopher, orator and poet, magician, alchemist and cabalist, friend (and enemy) of *letterati* and artists (Titian himself says he had done a portrait of him); much admired among French reformists, gambler and libertine at Venice; discoverer, by divine grace, of the miraculous invention that secured universal dominion over words and things [his theater of memory], that reveals, he writes, access to all the most beautiful secrets of the tradition of letters, Latin and vulgar. Giulio Camillo appears on first impression as one of those many charlatans, more or less ingenious, who between the Quattro and Cinquecento frequented the courts of Italy and Europe to earn themselves a livelihood."[60]

Near the end of his life Camillo dictated, on seven mornings, at Milan, a little work, *L'idea del theatro*, published at Venice and Florence in 1550. The text I have used is a photocopy of the original, from the rare book division of the National Library in Florence.[61] A reproduction can also be found, accompanied by a translation, in a Ph.D. dissertation done at the University of Pittsburgh.[62] It is Frances Yates who introduced Camillo and his theater to the contemporary reader, in two chapters of her incomparable *The Art of Memory*.[63] Yates includes a diagram of Camillo's theatre, showing all its parts.

Camillo's text is no more than a detailed description of the contents of the theater. The theater was built of wood, in Venice and in France, but neither survives. Camillo claimed that if one learned how to grasp the working of the theater one would have complete and perfect knowledge of all that could be known. He proposed to reveal its secret to the king of France. But when, apparently, he did not receive the monetary support he expected, he returned to Italy and accepted the offer of a pension, made by the Marchese del Vasto (Alfonso D'Avalos, the Spanish governor of Milan, who had been the patron of Ariosto), in return for Camillo teaching him the secret of the theater. Whether the Marchese received any such instruction is unclear.

While in France, it is reported, Camillo went with a group of dignitaries to see some wild animals. A lion escaped and came toward them. All fled except Camillo. He was of too great a bodily weight to run. The lion walked around him, rubbing against him and perhaps licking him, without harming him, until it was chased back to its place. Camillo declared that this was proof of his possession of "solar virtue." The lion is a solar animal; it recognized Camillo's corresponding divine nature.

Camillo's *L'idea del theatro* begins with the claim: "The most ancient and wisest writers have always had the habit of entrusting to their writings the secrets of God under obscure veils, so that they are not understood except by those who (as Christ says) have ears to hear, namely who by God are chosen to grasp his most sacred mysteries."[64] In issuing this warning, Camillo is echoing Plato's admonition to Dionysus of Syracuse, in his *Letters* (2.314), that he should not let his teaching be circulated among untrained people. Camillo is also echoing the warning of Hermes Trismegistus, in the prologue to the *Asclepius* in the *Hermetica*: "Call no one but Hammon lest the presence and interference of the many profane this most recent discourse on so great a subject, for the mind is irreverent that would make public, by the awareness of the many, a treatise so very full of the majesty of divinity."[65]

The *Zohar* of the Cabala contains a warning to those who would disclose secrets. The Bible is metaphorically described as a woman hidden under many veils who is revealed by lifting them one by one. Marsilio Ficino, in beginning his *Commentary on the Parmenides*, says: "Whoever is about to undertake the sacred reading of this work should first prepare himself by tempering his soul and freeing his intellect, before daring to take up the mysteries of this heavenly work."[66] Pico della Mirandola says, in his *Oration on the Dignity of Man*: "Then let us fill our well-prepared and purified soul with the light of natural philosophy, so that we may at last perfect her in the knowledge of things divine."[67] Those "who have ears to hear" are mentioned in Matthew (11:15), Mark (4:23), and Luke (8:8).

The theater was a system of word and thing, a complete metaphysics of memory. In it Camillo had produced the *clavis universalis*, the key to the alphabet of the world, whereby the grand book of all that there is could be read through the signs impressed by the divine mind. What Leibniz later sought through logic as *characteristica generalis*, Camillo discovered through poetic and rhetoric.

Camillo's theater was formed on seven grades, bisected by seven aisles or gangways that rose upwards from the stage. One entered on the stage and found oneself in the position of an actor, facing an "audience" composed of images (*pitture*) taken from Greco-Roman and Judeo-Christian mythology and religious texts. Yates gives a concise description of what anyone who enters the theater encounters: "Camillo's Theatre represents the universe expanding from First Causes through the stages of creation. First is the appearance of the simple elements from the waters on the Banquet grade; then the mixture of the elements in the Cave; then the creation of man's *mens* in the image of God on the grade of the Gorgon Sisters; then the union of man's soul and body on the grade of Pasiphe and the Bull; then the whole world of man's activities; his natural activities on the grade of the Sandals of Mercury; his arts and sciences, religion and laws on the Prometheus grade."[68]

Camillo's thesis is that all human knowledge derives from these archetypal, eternal images. They are the ultimate guides to all of human thought. By taking them up into our imagination, we acquire a basis from which we can bring forth a complete speech of the universe employing them as *topoi*. The seeker of knowledge who engages with the *pitture* would be able to see or behold (*theasthai*, from which the word *theater* is derived) the whole of human knowledge assembled in one place.

Yates says: "It is because he believes in the divinity of man that the divine Camillo makes his stupendous claim of being able to remember the universe by looking down upon it from above, from first causes, as though he were God. In this atmosphere, the relationship between man, the microcosm, and the world, the macrocosm, takes on a new significance. The microcosm can fully understand and fully remember the macrocosm, can hold it within his divine *mens* or memory."[69]

What is the secret of the theater? Here is a speculative answer. The secret is rhetoric: the rhetoric of the complete speech. The person entering Camillo's theater on the stage encounters the archetypal images from which all of human thought derives. The *pitture* give access to the Platonic *eidē*, the ideas or forms that as such are to be seen fully and only with the mind's eye. The theater is a machine that allows the individual's human *mens* to align itself with the images of the contents of the divine *mens*. The individual, after great study, extending over many months or perhaps years, can proceed to compose a speech of the whole of human experience in accord with the five divisions of classical rhetoric: *Inventio* (Invention), *Dispositio* (Disposition), *Elocutio* (Elocution), *Memoria* (Memory), and *Pronuntiatio* (Delivery).

Inventio is the collecting of materials on a subject. In the theater, Camillo has already accomplished this. Nothing is left out. All of the forms of the human world are there. They are the master *topoi* from which a comprehensivee speech of the human world can be put forth. *Dispositio* is the arrangement of these *topoi* into an order that satisfies the imagination and reason. Camillo's *dispositio* reflects Vitruvius, *On Architecture*. Vitruvius says: "Now architecture consists of Order. . . . Order is the balanced adjustment of the details of the work separately, and, as to the whole, the arrangement of the proportion with a view to a symmetrical result. . . . Arrangement [*Dispositio*], however, is the fit assemblage of details, and, arising from this assemblage, the elegant effect of the work and its dimensions, along with a certain quality or character" (1.2.2). The key to *dispositio* is proportion and proportion is the center of the secret. Proportion as a way of grasping ideas must be learned in order to acquire the mastery necessary for thinking by means of the theater.

Elocutio is the expression of these *topoi* in language. This act is accomplished by study of the works of Cicero that Camillo stored in the coffers and drawers in the theater. Cicero is the greatest of all orators. It is from Cicero that elocution can be learned. *Memoria* requires that the master images of the theater can be accessed by mentally moving up each of the seven gangways from the first causes of the world to the Promethean grade. The author of the *Ad herennium* says: "Now let me turn to the treasure-house of the ideas supplied by Invention, to the guardian of all the parts of rhetoric, the Memory" (3.6.28). The author says further:

"Those who know the letters of the alphabet can thereby write out what is dictated to them and read aloud what they have written. Likewise, those who have learned mnemonics can set in *loci* [Greek *topoi*] what they have heard, and from these *loci* deliver it by memory. For the *loci* are very much like wax tablets or papyrus, the images like the letters, the arrangement and disposition of the images like the script, and the delivery is like the reading" (3.7.30).

Pronuntiatio allows the adept to draw forth from the theater whatever is needed to speak on any particular subject. The ground for comprehending any consequent is at the disposal of whoever has mastered the contents and order of the theater and who can imitate well the oratory of Cicero. It is at the level of *Pronuntiatio* that one fully educated in the theater can demonstrate wisdom on any subject. Whoever is fully learned in the theater can speak with eloquence on any particular subject and on the human world as a whole. Such a person can enact the ideal of the Renaissance: to be wisdom speaking—*la sapienza che parla*.

Since Camillo's declaration in the first sentence of his *L'idea del theatro* makes a distinction between the many and the few, he could presume that the many would regard his theater as no more than a curiosity. But the few would grasp its true nature and realize the genius that was hidden within its walls. Camillo's theater of memory is itself a complicated *topos* that, once encountered, enters the visitor's memory. Once it is encountered, its fascination persists. It connects the memory that holds together the human self with the memory that holds humanity together.

12. Giambattista Vico, Fantasia

Giambattista Vico (1668-1744) described himself as "choleric to a fault" (*Egli peccò nella collera*). He said that he publicly confessed this failing. He regarded his greatest achievement to be his discovery and presentation of his *Scienza nuova*. But he found that his ideas were not well received. He says: "Among the caitiff semi-learned or pseudo-learned, the more shameless called him a fool, or in somewhat more courteous terms they said that he was obscure or eccentric and had odd ideas." His response to these detractors was to withdraw to his desk, "as to his high impregnable citadel." Despite the adversities he experienced, Vico said he "held himself more fortunate than Socrates."[70]

Vico was the new Socrates of the new city—Neapolis. His agora was all of history, such that he is now considered as the founder of the modern conception of the philosophy of history. Although Vico lived in the eighteenth century, the "age of Enlightenment," he is often regarded as the culmination of the Renaissance. Karl-Otto Apel, in *Die Idee der Sprache in der Tradition des Humanismus von Dante bis Vico* (The idea of language in the tradition of humanism from Dante to Vico), called Vico the "Owl of Minerva" of Renaissance Humanistic culture, referring to Hegel's image in the Preface to *Grundlinien der Philosophie des Rechts*, that the "*Eule der Minerva*," the owl of wisdom, takes flight at the falling of the dusk.[71]

The third edition (1744) of Vico's masterpiece has the title: *Principi di scienza nuova di Giambattista Vico d'intorno alla comune natura delle nazioni—Principles of New Science of Giambattista Vico concerning the Common Nature of the Nations.*[72] In the *Digest of Justinian*, the compilation of Roman law, which Vico regarded as a complete statement of human wisdom, a distinction is made regarding three senses of law: *jus naturale*, *jus gentium*, and *jus civile*. *Jus* is derived from *justitia*, which is the art of goodness and fairness. What the Greeks knew as philosophia, the Romans knew as *jurisprudentia*.

Jus civile is positive law that varies from nation to nation. *Jus naturale* is "that which nature has taught to all animals, for it is not a law specific to humankind but is common to all animals—land animals, sea animals, and the birds as well." A prime example is the union of male and female and the procreation and rearing of offspring, which among human beings are the basis of marriage. "*Jus gentium*, the law of nations, is that which all human peoples observe. That it is not co-extensive with natural law can be grasped easily, since this latter is common to all animals whereas *jus gentium* is common only to human beings among themselves" (1.1.4).

Vico transposes *jus gentium* into his conception of *storia ideal eterna* (ideal eternal history). This history is "traversed in time by the histories of all nations" (393). All nations pass through three ages—an age of gods, an age of heroes, and an age of humans. The age of gods is one in which all of nature is seen as full of gods. The age of heroes is one in which the virtues by which social life is conducted are conceived through the images of heroic figures. The age of humans is one in which social order depends upon governments and rational forms of order. Within the course of these three ages is a sequence of each nation experiencing "its rise, development, maturity, decline, and fall" (245), such that: "Human beings first feel necessity, then look for utility, next attend to comfort, still later amuse themselves with pleasure, thence grow dissolute in luxury, and finally go mad and waste their substance [*finalmente impazzano in istrappazzar le sostanze*]" (241). One thinks here of Stephen's statement in Joyce's *Ulysses*: "History is a nightmare from which I am trying to awake."[73] It was said that Vico looks at history and never smiles. His truth is a truth governed by Saturn, a melancholy truth.

Vico says that all nations, barbarous as well as civilized, "keep these three human customs: all have some religion, all contract solemn marriages, all bury their dead" (333). These are the three principles that define humanity.

When society replaces religion with politics, considers marriage as no more than a convention, separate from procreation and the rearing of children, and loses the sense of the sanctity of life that is engendered by witnessing and participating in the ceremony of burial, people lose their humanity. Vico says: "For religions alone can bring the peoples to do virtuous works by appeal to their feelings, which alone move people to perform them; and the reasoned maxims of the philosophers concerning virtue are of use only when employed by a good eloquence for kindling the feelings to do the duties of virtue" (1110).

Vico sees his own nation as undergoing a *corso* and a *ricorso*. The age of gods and the age of heroes of its *corso* occur among the very early Greeks and are recorded in Homer's poems. After Homer, when the philosophers arrive, it is the beginning of the third age, which ends with the fall of Rome. The first age of the *ricorso* is marked by a return to religion—what from the perspective of the Renaissance Humanists were the "dark ages." The High Middle Ages correspond to the age of heroes. Here the heroes are not Achilles and Odysseus; they are those following the ideals of knighthood. Dante is the summary figure of the first two ages of the *ricorso*. Vico calls Dante "the Tuscan Homer" (786).

After Dante come the philosophers of the Renaissance, who find their sources in Greek and Roman thought. From there develops the life and mentality of the moderns. "For such peoples, like so many beasts, have fallen into the custom of each person thinking only of private interests until such persons have reached the extreme of delicacy, or better of pride in which like wild animals they bristle and lash out at the slightest displeasure. . . . In this way, through long centuries of barbarism, rust will consume the misbegotten subtleties of malicious wits that have turned them into beasts made more inhuman by the barbarism of reflection than the first humans had been made by the barbarism of sense" (1106). Vico finds himself living among barbarians. We can live among barbarians only by understanding the providential order expressed in the ideal eternal history that provides us with the knowledge of events necessary for the practice of prudence.

The three ages of ideal eternal history that each nation undergoes is a jurisprudence of the human race. It is a conception of the *jus gentium* placed in time. Vico says: "Doctrines must take their beginning from that of the matters of which they treat" (314). The law of the three ages rests on an account of what is common to the nations. Vico says: "But in the night of thick darkness enveloping the earliest antiquity, so remote from ourselves, there shines the eternal and never failing light of a truth beyond all question: that the world of civil society has certainly been made by human beings, and that its principles are therefore to be found within the modifications of our own human mind" (331). Vico says: "It is evident that the entire original human race was divided into two species: the one of giants, the other of human beings of normal stature; the former gentiles, the latter Hebrews" (172).

Following the universal flood, two of the three sons of Noah—Ham and Japeth—wandered the great forest of the earth. Over two centuries the offspring of these sons became giants, who later founded the gentile nations. The third son of Noah, Shem, and his offspring, settled in East Asia, where they preserved the religion of Noah, remained of normal stature, and became the ancient Hebrews. The giants were motivated wholly by bodily sensation. "They were, so to speak, all body" (570). As the world dried from the flood, the giants experienced a new phenomenon—thunder and lightning—which made them for the first time aware of the sky, and it instilled a primal fear or terror (*spavento*) in them.

The giants: "expressed their very violent passions by shouting [*urlando*] and grumbling [*brontolando*], they pictured the sky to themselves as a great animated body, which in that aspect they called Jove" (377). *Urlare* is to howl like an animal or to shout like a human; *brontolare* is to grumble or to rumble (as does thunder). The giants were part human and part beast. Human speech was first formed through onomatopoeia, through "introjections, which are sounds articulated under the impetus of violent passions. . . . These introjections of Jove should give birth to one produced by the human voice: *pa*!; and that this should then be doubled: *pape*!" (448). The giants formed Jove "by virtue of a wholly corporeal imagination [*corpolentissima fantasia*]" (376). Their bodies trembled, as does the thunderous sky. Jove is the first name. Once one thing is named, all things can be named, resulting in articulated speech.

Memory originates at the same time as speech. Vico says, "memory is the same as imagination [*la memoria è la stessa che la fantasia*]." Vico says further: "Memory has three different aspects: memory [*memoria*] when it remembers things, imagination [*fantasia*] when it alters or imitates them, and ingenuity [*ingegno*] when it gives them a new turn or puts them into proper arrangement and relationship [*le contorna e pone in acconcezza ed assettamento*]." Vico adds: "For these reasons the theological poets called Memory the mother of the Muses" (819).

For the giants, every instance of thunder was originally a unique occurrence, a sequence of sheer particulars. But when suddenly they apprehended the thunder as Jove, they were able to grasp that each occurrence of thunder was the occurrence of a single phenomenon—what they named Jove. This grasping of thunder is an act of memory. The separate occurrences of thunder are held in memory and then grasped as one thing. Vico says: "We can now scarcely understand and cannot at all imagine [*immaginare*] how the first human beings thought who founded gentile humanity. For their minds were so limited to particulars that they regarded every change of facial expression as a new face" (700).

Fantasia as a Vichian term is different from *immaginazione*. *Immaginazione* forms a sense impression into an image of something that is held in memory and that can then be an object of thought. *Fantasia* as Vico employs it is the power by which the mind originally forms the object itself. The difference between these two senses of "imagination" underlies Vico's "imaginative universals" (*universali fantastici*). The first humans form their world through imaginative universals. The apprehension of the world in terms of imaginative universals is accomplished in poetic characters. Vico says: "We find that the principle of these origins both of languages and letters lies in the fact that the first gentile peoples, by a demonstrated necessity of nature, were poets who spoke in poetic characters. This discovery, which is the master key of this Science, has cost us the persistent research of almost all our literary life, because with our civilized natures we [moderns] cannot at all imagine [*immaginare*] and can understand only by great toil the poetic nature of these first human beings" (34).

Vico's concept of *universali fantastici* that are accomplished through the speech of poetic characters is a more fundamental concept of metaphor than the traditional concept of metaphor that derives from Aristotle's *Poetics*. Aristotle says: "Metaphor consists in giving the thing a name that belongs to something else; the transference being either from genus to species, or from species to genus, or from species to species, or on grounds of analogy" (1457b).

Jove, the first imaginative universal, is not the result of asserting an analogy of thunder as a physical occurrence to Jove as a divine being formed in thought. Jove *is* thunder. Jove is not *like* thunder. Jove is brought into being *as* thunder. This Vichian sense of metaphor underlies the traditional sense of metaphor and is presupposed by it.

Poetic characters are expressed in fables and are the basis of fables. Vico says: "Every metaphor so formed is a fable in brief" (404). Fables are metaphors expanded into narratives. Fables or myths are statements of the original truths of the gentile nations. Vico says: "So that, if we consider the matter well, poetic truth is metaphysical truth, and physical truth which is not in conformity with it should be considered false. Thence springs this important consideration in poetic theory: the true war chief, for example, is the Godfrey that Torquato Tasso represents [*finge*]; and all the chiefs who do not conform throughout to Godfrey are not true chiefs of war" (205). Each chief *is* equally Godfrey and Godfrey is Godfrey.

Memory is not only the essential element in the generation of human speech, it is also the basis of Vico's new science itself. Vico says: "Our Science therefore comes to describe at the same time an ideal eternal history traversed in time by the history of every nation in its rise, development, maturity, decline, and fall. Indeed, we make bold to affirm that he who meditates this Science narrates to himself this ideal eternal history so far as he himself makes it for himself by that proof 'it had, has, and will have to be [*dovette, deve, dovrà*]'" (349). The proof of this science rests on our ability to incorporate the art of the Muses into our own thought. The song of the Muses shows us how to think in terms of time. Our grasp of ideal eternal history transforms the development of the great city of nations from a contingent sequence to a necessary sequence, such as we attain through recollection, not as a process simply of remembering.

The method by which we come to comprehend the common nature of the nations is the same as that through which we can come to comprehend ourselves. In describing his autobiography, Vico says: "And, as may be seen, he wrote it as a philosopher, meditating the causes, natural and moral, and the occasions of fortune; why even from childhood he had felt an inclination for certain studies and an aversion from others; what opportunities and obstacles had advanced or retarded his progress; and lastly the effect of his own exertions in right directions, which were destined later to bear fruit in those reflections on which he built his final work, the *New Science*, which was to demonstrate that his intellectual life was bound to have been such as it was and not otherwise."[74] Vico's autobiography accords with the principles employed in his new science. His autobiography is the ideal eternal history of himself. He comes to know himself in the same way he comes to know the great city of the human race as having a providential order. It is Vico's philosophy of self-knowledge.

13. G. W. F. Hegel, Er-Innerung

Georg Wilhelm Friedrich Hegel (1770-1831) identified himself on the title page of his *Phänomenologie des Geistes—Phenomenology of Spirit* (1807) as "Dr. and Professor of Philosophy at Jena, Assessor in the Jena Ducal Mineralogical Society and member of other learned associations." Hegel had been inducted into the Jena Mineralogical Society in January 1804, and was issued a pass in May by the University for a field trip to Göttingen and the Harz Mountains for geological study. However, Hegel makes no specific mention of mineralogical science in the *Phenomenology* or any of his subsequent writings, including his discussion of the natural sciences in his *Encyklopädie* (3rd ed. 1830).

In his early work, *Differenz des Fichte'schen und Schelling'schen Systems der Philosophie* (1801), Hegel identified himself as "*der Weltweisheit Doktor*" (Doctor of Worldly Wisdom). Hegel mentions *Weltweisheit* later in his career, in his discussion of the "Concept of Religion" in his *Lectures on the Philosophy of Religion*, in which he contrasts *Weltweisheit* with *Heiligkeit* (Holiness). It seems likely that Hegel regarded himself as the Dr. of Worldly Wisdom throughout his career, but his career as a mineralogist seems confined to his early years at Jena.

Without question, the *Phänomenologie des Geistes* is the most difficult book to read in the history of philosophy.[75] In a letter to Johann Heinrich Voss of May 1805, Hegel wrote: "Luther made the *Bible*, you have made Homer speak German—the greatest gift that can be made to a people . . . so I say of my own endeavor, that I wish to attempt to teach philosophy to speak German."[76] Hegel's task is much different from that of Luther or Voss, who were translating meanings from one language to another. Hegel must elicit philosophical meanings from the natural language of German, much in the way Socrates does from Greek. Hegel stands in contrast to Kant, whose *Kritik der reinen Vernunft (Critique of Pure Reason)*, although written in German, depends entirely on Latin terminology. Hegel employs ordinary German words with active meanings. He does not resort to framing his thought in a technical vocabulary.

Hegel's *Phenomenology* shows us a way to think through—to systematic recollect—the fundamental forms by which human consciousness develops. Hegel says: "The science of this journey is the science of the *experience* that consciousness undergoes [*Die Wissenschaft dieses Wegs ist Wissenschaft der* Erfahrung, *die das Bewußtsein macht*]" (36;

p.32). The *Phenomenology* begins with the experience of consciousness, with the sensuous apprehension of what consciousness finds present before it as something "here" and "now." The *Phenomenology* ends with the experience consciousness attains of its object and itself as "absolute knowing" (*absolutes Wissen*). In between are episodes and stages, with names such as: the inverted world; masterhood and servitude; the unhappy consciousness; craniology; virtue and the way of the world; the spiritual menagerie, humbug, or the thing itself; absolute freedom and terror; the beautiful soul, evil and its forgiveness; the living work of art; God as light; and revealed religion.

Hegel's science of the experience of consciousness does not begin where consciousness itself begins. Cassirer recognizes this point in the Preface to the second volume of his *Philosophy of Symbolic Forms: Mythical Thought*. Cassirer shows that the sphere of sensation develops from the sphere of mythical thought. Cassirer says: "For the actual point of departure for all science, the immediacy from which it starts, lies not so much in the sensory sphere as in the sphere of mythical intuition. . . . Before self-consciousness rises to this abstraction, it lives in the world of the mythical consciousness, a world not of 'things' and their 'attributes' but of mythical potencies and powers, of demons and gods. If then, in accordance with Hegel's demand, science is to provide the natural consciousness with a ladder leading to itself, it must first set this ladder a step lower."[77]

Hegel labels the first stage of his phenomenology "sensory certainty" (*sinnliche Gewißheit*). The key word is "certainty." Where Hegel's phenomenology begins, consciousness has already emerged from the world experienced as an interplay of benign and malignant forces of light and dark, into a world of neutral sensed particulars. The mentality of sensory certainty has within it an element of scepticism, not Scepticism as Hegel will develop it later, as a stage of consciousness corresponding to a philosophical position that is a response to Stoicism, but scepticism as present in ordinary common sense—the ability to doubt what the object seems to be. The corrective to such doubt is the immediate sensing of what is before the mind. What is sensed is true. Only when judgment is introduced can the truth of what is sensed be evaluated.

The truth of sensation is the first attempt of consciousness at absolute knowing. It is the first step in the quest for certainty in which consciousness can engage. Mythical thought is thought confined to the level of the primordial formation of sensation. Scepticism does not occur as an element of mythical thought. The world is just as it is felt. Once the question of certainty is raised, consciousness seeks to find what is indubitable. It seeks to obtain a mode of absolute knowing. Hegel's progression of the phenomena of consciousness demonstrates that within each attempt by consciousness to attain absolute knowing there is an internal dialectic that is unresolved, but that leads consciousness to formulate itself in a further way. Consciousness finds that the internal dialectic carries it into a new form. The opposition that consciousness seeks to overcome and possess the certainty of absolute knowing has not been reached.

The principle of this internal dialectic is present in the unique German verb, *aufheben*. When consciousness affirms one side of an opposition and denies the other, the other is not without content. The truth of one side of an opposition is true only when placed against what is denied as true. All trues are partially false and partially true. Hegel says *aufheben "ist ein* Negieren *und ein* Aufbewahren *zugleich* [is a *negating* and a *preserving* at once]" (113; p.90). The principle of *aufheben* allows Hegel to overcome the ancient sceptical sense of dialectic, in which dialectic is regarded as a flat movement between pro and con, a simple back and forth of thought, leaving thought with a pendulum of opposition in which the possibility of movement toward certainty is eliminated.

The double sense of *aufheben* allows thought and consciousness itself to move from one side of an opposition, from which something of its truth is denied, to the other, from which something of its truth is preserved and is brought back to reconceive the truth of the original. This is the process that Hegel describes in his conception of the *spekulativer Satz*—the speculative sentence—in which the meaning of the subject is to be found in the predicate. But once thought has moved to the predicate, the meaning of the predicate depends upon its connection to the subject. By bringing the predicate back into connection with the subject, the meaning of the subject is changed and enriched. In this way, Hegel says, a harmony is brought forth (61; p.51). And in this way thought proceeds toward the True that is the whole (*Das Wahre ist das Ganze*) (20; p.21).

In the final paragraph of the *Phenomenology*, Hegel reveals that the self-development of consciousness has been nothing more than a Gallery of Images (*eine Galerie von Bildern*) (808; p.563). The illusion of each stage is that it has accomplished a synthesis of the opposites that lie within it—the version of in-itself and for-itself that it inherits from the previous stage. Absolute knowing is reached when consciousness accepts the fact that each side of the particular opposition inherent in each stage of consciousness cannot be more than a correspondence to the other—can only be *entsprechend*. At no stage can the opposition be merged into one, into a unity. The "and" (*und*) that stands between in-itself (*an-sich*) and for-itself (*für-sich*) must be accepted as the abiding condition of the experience of the human spirit. Each stage of consciousness is no more than a particular version of *Anundfürsichsein* (25; p.24). The acceptance of the permanence of "and" (*und*) is the fundamental condition of human wisdom. Absolute knowing accepts things as they are. What is, is to be grasped only in terms of an internal opposition.

In concluding the *Phenomenology*, Hegel employs *Erinnerung* (recollection) four times. The first sense of *Erinnerung* is spirit (*Geist*) becoming history. Consciousness can recollect the course it has undergone as the experience of being in time. The second sense of *Erinnerung* is stated as "*Er-Innerung*." On this sense of absolute knowing, Ernst Bloch remarks: "In Hegel's *Phenomenology* one notices quite frequently how a sudden linguistic insight is inextricably bound up with true philosophical invention. This occurs when Hegel separates the word recollection [*Er-Innerung*] and thereby takes recollection (as the condition of history) into the most interior, the most subjectivistic opposition to 'estrangement' [*Entäusserung*] (as the condition of nature). Naturally, this inward, self-returning, subjectivistic sense of the word recollection would not have been usable if the concept [*Begriff*] had not been the guiding factor in the matter; but a reciprocal action of the inventions nonetheless exists."[78]

The hyphenation is an act of genius on Hegel's part. It calls the reader's attention to the fact that *Erinnerung* is the master key for comprehending how to read the *Phenomenology* as a process of the inwardizing of the self. Human beings, by their nature, have an interior life, as opposed to the life of non-human beings that, by their nature, do not have an interior sense of their existence. Thus human nature is not an estrangement from nature, rather, it is a fulfillment of it.

The third sense of *Erinnerung* calls attention to the fact that consciousness not only realizes that each of the stages it depicts to itself is itself, the forms of its inner life, but that, to know each stage, consciousness must enter into the internal life of each stage. Consciousness cannot know each stage simply as an object. Consciousness must see itself as existing in each stage. Each stage must be grasped as something that is both in and for itself. Hegel's work is a colossus of systematic memory.

The fourth sense of *Erinnerung* is the realization that consciousness can never complete the science of itself. There will always be a further stage of development, a new set of oppositions, beyond those in the past that it recollects. These two senses of recollection, taken together, Hegel says, are the "Golgotha of absolute spirit" (*die Schädelstätte des absoluten Geist*). Consciousness then acquires the perspective on experience that corresponds to that of divine vision. Hegel's last words of the *Phenomenology* are a paraphrase of a couplet of Schiller's poem "Friendship": "From the chalice of his realm of spirits / Foams forth for Him his own infinitude." The whole can never be fully expressed. Consciousness can never complete itself, never complete the whole. Its self-knowledge is always in the making. When consciousness attains this perspective, the human spirit realizes the perpetual incompleteness of itself.

Absolute knowing is not an act of the synthesis of opposites. It is a way of thinking that accepts the fact that all experience occurs through opposition, and never fully overcomes the opposition that is within what is human. Absolute knowing is the art of the Muses. Hegel, in a fragment, calls Mnemosyne "the absolute Muse" (*die absolute Muse*).[79] Absolute knowing is certain that the whole is a circle within which consciousness is unceasingly configuring and reconfiguring itself, and in so doing recollecting and re-collecting itself. Like Plato, Hegel sees everything twice—once, with the bodily eye, as phenomena that are preserved in memory as a gallery of images, and then, with the mind's eye, as the subjects of thought that are expressed in the progression of categories in the *Wissenschaft der Logik*, that completes the second part of Hegel's system of philosophical science. In the *Science of Logic* Hegel says: "The concept of pure science and its deduction [its justification, *quid iuris*] is therefore presupposed in the present work in so far as the *Phenomenology of Spirit* is nothing other than that deduction."[80]

Hegel says that this final form of spirit that is absolute knowing is what self-knowledge is. Hegel says: "This last shape of spirit—the spirit which at the same time gives its complete and true content the form of the Self and thereby realizes its concept while remaining in its concept [*Begriff*] in this realization—is absolute knowing; it is spirit knowing itself in the spirit-shape, or *conceptual knowing*. The truth is not only *in itself* completely equal to certainty, but it also has the *shape* of certainty of itself, or it is in its existence [*Dasein*], i.e., for the knowing spirit is the *form* of self-knowledge" (798; p.556).

Having begun with the certainty of sensation, consciousness ends its journey through the forms of itself with the certainty of itself, as the whole of itself, the self that has become *Geist*. This is a certainty that only recollection can bring. What we recollect is what we are. It requires the art of the Muses to be turned into the science of the experience of consciousness. This science produces a certainty of Self that allows philosophy to put aside the element of scepticism that always lies in wait when self-consciousness pursues the love of wisdom.

14. James Joyce, "mememormee!"

I turn again to Joyce. Earlier I considered his sense of humor, of the joke and its connection to satire. I look back again on *Finnegans Wake* as a theater of memory, a receptacle that holds Joyce's humor, and how we may find ourselves within this receptacle, on this stage. Joyce's dedication to the circle, of circling the square of the four books of *Finnegans Wake*, is manifest in the circle of the text as beginning with the last half of a sentence, the first half of which appears as the last words of the work.

Let us consider the part of the text, in the middle of which is "mememormee!" "O bitter ending! I'll slip away before they're up. They'll never see. Nor know. Nor miss me. And it's old and old it's sad and old it's sad and weary I go back to you, my cold father, my cold mad father, my cold mad feary father, till the near sight of the mere size of him, the moyles and moyles of it, moananoaning, makes me seasilt saltsick and I rush, my only, into your arms. I see them rising! Save me from those therrble prongs! Two more. Onetwo moremens more. So. Avelaval. My leaves have drifted from me. All. But one clings still. I'll bear it on me. To remind me of. Lff! So soft this morning ours. Yes. Carry me along, taddy, like you done through the toy fair. If I seen him bearing down on me now under whitespread wings like he'd come from Arkangels, I sink I'd die down over his feet, humbly dumbly, only to washup. Yes, tid. There's where. First. We pass through grass behush the bush to. Whish! A gull. Gulls. Far calls. Coming, far! End here. Us then. Finn, again! Take. Bussoftlhee, mememormee! Till thousendsthee. Lps. The keys to. Given! A way a lone a last a loved a long the [ ] riverrun, past Eve and Adam's, from swerve of shore to bend of bay, brings us by a commodius vicus of recirculation back to Howth Castle and Environs" (627.34-003.03).

In the stanzas of the last Canto of *Paradiso*, in the *Divina Commedia*, Dante emerges from his journey to return to the mortal world:

> O Light Eternal fixed in itself alone,
>   by Itself alone understood, which from Itself
>   loves and glows, self-knowing and self-known;
>
> that second aureole which shone forth in Thee,
>   conceived as a reflection of the first—
>   or which appeared so to my scrutiny—

> seemed in Itself of Its own coloration
>   to be painted with man's image. I fixed my eyes
>   on that alone in rapturous contemplation.
>
> Like a geometer wholly dedicated
>   to squaring the circle, but who cannot find,
>   think as he may, the principle indicated—
>
> so did I study the supernal face.
>   I yearned to know just how our image merges
>   into that circle, and how it there finds place;
>
> but mine were not the wings for such a flight.
>   Yet, as I wished, the truth I wished for came
>   cleaving my mind in a great flash of light.
>
> Here my powers rest from their high fantasy,
>   but already I could feel my being turned—
>   instinct and intellect balanced equally
>
> as in a wheel whose motion nothing jars—
> by the Love that moves the Sun and the other stars.

Dante, in his attempt to see how "our image" is encircled by the divine light, finds that he is unable to grasp the principle necessary to understand how this occurs. He is like the geometer who is unable to find the principle by which the circle could be squared. The quadrature of the circle is a problem as old as Anaxagoras and satirized by Aristophanes in *Birds* (1001-1005). It was a problem pursued in mathematical works from ancient Greece forward, until Ferdinand von Lindemann in 1882, working from the proof that e could not be a root of quadratic equation with rational coefficients and from the proof of the transcendence of e, proved the transcendence of π. Joyce, as mentioned above, did not attempt to square the circle, but instead circled the square—"circling the square" (186.12).

Dante enters his journey from the mortal world into the underworld with the words:

> Midway in our life's journey, I went astray
>   from the straight road and woke to find myself
>   alone in a dark wood. How shall I say
>
> what wood that was! I never saw so dear,
>   so rank, so arduous a wilderness!
>   Its very memory [*che nel pensier*] gives a shape to fear.

In the second Canto Dante calls upon the Muses, the daughters of Memory, to come to his aid:

> O Muses! O High Genius [*ingegno*]! Be my aid!
> O Memory [*mente*], recorder of the vision,
> here shall your true nobility be displayed![81]

Dante leaves the mortal world to discover what is beyond it. He does not do so as an act of will. He awakens into it, and finally returns to the mortal world with the memory of what is beyond it. The reader of Joyce's *Finnegans Wake*, beginning with the half sentence, enters its dream world and finally, over six-hundred pages later, begins to exit it and then realizes that the exit is only part of a circle that takes one back again into "a commodius vicus of recirculation." The announcement, to remember me, becomes a declaration, pronounced just before re-entry into the world of the dream, governed by Vico's *corso* and *ricorso*, which run through all human events.

Behind Joyce's "mememormee" is the Greek word *mnēmē*—a remembrance, memory, record of a person or thing. It also refers to memory as a power of the mind. It is the word used by Hesiod in the *Theogony*. As Joyce says: "And it's old and old it's sad and old." To ask to be remembered is sad. We might amplify the sadness of the request to be remembered with: "It seems so long since, ages since. As if you had been long far away Afartodays, afeartonights, and me as with you in thadark. You will tell me some time if I can believe its all. You know where I am bringing you? You remember?" (622.13-17). Joyce's "mememormee!" is a "twone" (003.12), a "Onetwo" (628.05). Its double meaning is both to remember me and that I am memory. All that I am is stored in my memory. Memory is always a circle. We enter memory only to come back to where we were, just as we do in *Finnegans Wake* and as we do with Dante in the *Divine Comedy*. We are the circle of memory that we enact. It contains the knowledge that we have of ourselves. In it is all of the individual self that remembers and all of the humanity that we have been able to incorporate into ourselves through our humane education.

In the *Divine Comedy*, Dante shows us every one of the conditions of human existence, from the lost souls in the Bolgias of the *Inferno* to the souls on the shore and slope of *Purgatorio* to the blessed spheres of *Paradiso*. In *Finnegans Wake* Joyce will show us what language itself is, as the distinctive power of the human mind. We are confronted with words from many languages but, above all, with words from the four major European languages in which Joyce was fluent, spoken in the four cities that span Joyce's career, Dublin, Trieste, Paris, and Zurich—

English, Italian, French, and German—with the addition of Latin. The reader needs to know these languages to grasp the language of *Finnegans Wake*. They are the basis of its music. "Are we speachin d'anglas landadge or are you sprakin sea Djoytsch?" (485.12-13).

Finnegans Wake is a prose poem, not a novel. It has none of the characteristics of a novel. Archibald MacLeish concludes his poem, *Ars Poetica*: "A poem should not mean / But be."[82] It is the right definition with which to approach both Joyce's and Dante's poems. They spread human existence out before us, for us to see. We need not ask what they mean. They are us. Like other poems of this order, like those of Homer and the *Aeneid* of Virgil, they prompt our memory to seek out the nature of the human, and in so doing they take us to the speculative reason of philosophy, of figures like Plato, who is influenced by Homer, and Hegel, who is influenced by Schiller, and Vico, who is influenced by Dante.

In *Ulysses*, at the beginning of the Nestor episode, there is the line: "Fabled by the daughters of memory. And yet it was in some way if not as memory fabled it."[83] Then a mention of Blake, likely to *A Vision of the Last Judgment*: "Fable or Allegory is Form'd by the daughters of Memory." Joyce said, regarding the "nightlong" (184.07), the "nightmaze" (411.08) of *Finnegans Wake*: "In my imitation of the dream-state, I effect in a few minutes what it has sometimes taken centuries to bring about."[84] The dream and the fable are our access to what is stored in memory. Our access to what we experienced in a dream is precarious because, as we pass from the dream to being awake, we often immediately forget what was in the dream. The fable is continually present and can state a truth that can be stated in no other way. Our guides are the Muses, who give the poet as well as us access to memory. It is Calliope who leads us, because as Hesiod says, she is the "Beautiful Voiced" and the "greatest of them all" (*Th.* 79). In the first Canto of *Purgatorio*, Dante says:

> Yours am I, sacred Muses! To you I pray.
>   Here let dead poetry rise once more to life,
>   and here let sweet Calliope rise and play
>
> some fair accompaniment in that high strain
>   whose power the wretched Pierides once felt
>   so terribly they dared not hope again.

Poetry is metaphysical. The poetic imagination does in images what reason does conceptually. In the final sentence of *Modes of Thought*, Alfred North Whitehead says: "Poetry allies itself to metre, philosophy to mathematic pattern."[85] The poet, like Dante, has glimpsed the Mount of Joy (*dilettosso monte*), looking past the three beasts that would block his way—the spotted Leopard (*lonza*), the great Lion (*leone*), and the She-Wolf (*lupa*). With Virgil's guidance, Dante finds a way to circumvent these beasts and begin his journey toward *Paradiso*. The speculative philosopher, the metaphysician, has, with Hegel, glimpsed the presence of the Absolute, existing as a form of knowing that places all lesser forms of the human spirit in memory. Joyce has glimpsed what is beyond the "nightmaze": "Lff! So soft this morning ours. Yes. Carry me along, taddy, like you done through the toy fair." And then, "Far calls. Coming, far! End here. Us then. Finn, again! Take. Bussoftlhee, mememormee!"

We must circle back and go through things again. But this time we know how to have "Two thinks at a time." We know that all that is in experience is a "twone." Like Finnegan, we are all dead and alive at the same time. Every moment of our life is one of the moments of our death. Our life, then, is a wake that is self-conducted, a wake that is repeated every day, as every morning turns into every evening. Every morning is a resurrection from the night world of the dream, only we find ourselves, every evening, again "Beside the rivering waters of, hitherandthithering waters of. Night!" (216.04-05).

Joyce has explained self-knowledge to us. We are creatures of memory. What we are is what we can recollect of ourselves and put together as a narrative. That narrative is our narrative, but it is a narrative of all that we have absorbed of the memory of humanity that we have accumulated in our education. What we can say to ourselves depends upon what we have found in the litter of the human world at large. For Joyce, from litter comes letter comes literature. The literature of self is our self-knowledge. We are no more and no less than our autobiography.

Epilogue

The Florentine historian and statesman Francesco Guicciardini, in his *Ricordi*, says: "All that which has been in the past and is at present will be again in the future. But both the names and the appearances of things change, so that he who does not have a good eye will not recognize them. Nor will he know how to grasp a norm of conduct or make a judgment by means of observation."[86] In his statement Guicciardini brings together the wisdom of the Muses with the wisdom of Ecclesiastes: "What has been is what will be, and what has been done is what will be done; there is nothing new under the sun. Is there a thing of which it is said, 'See this is new'? It has already been, in the ages before us" (1.9-10).

To act with decorum, with dignity and decency, depends on good character. Character is formed and sustained by habit. Faced with a moral choice, we act from character. Our judgment derives from what we can recollect of what has gone before in similar circumstances and what we can envision of the future. Our choice, directed by correct reason, implements the particular virtue that applies to the circumstances in which our choice is to be made. Once we have acted, we must consider the degree to which we have achieved the Good. When we encounter a similar situation in the future in which a moral choice must be made, what we recollect of past choices and our assessment of them will guide our present choice. Morality is an art based on our power of memory. Like any art, its achievement is attained through practice. We learn morality the way an art is learned.

In making moral choices, we can look to human culture for precedent, especially to the law. As in the law, we can seek out precedent. Precedents can go back as far as the *Code of Laws* of the rule of Hammurabi in the first dynasty of Babylon, and the *Law of the Twelve Tables* in the early Roman Republic. We can look to the *Iliad* and *Odyssey* of Homer, the *Divine Comedy* of Dante, to the plays of Shakespeare from the tragedies of *Hamlet* and *King Lear* to *A Midsummer Night's Dream* and *All's Well That Ends Well*, to Goethe's *Faust: Parts One and Two* and his bildungsroman, *Wilhelm Meister*.

We can look to the *Hebrew Bible* and the *New Testament*, to the *Qur'ān, Upanishads, Bhagavadgītā, Tibetan Book of the Dead (Bardo Thödol), Lankavatara Sutra, Analects*, and to the *I Ching or Book of Changes*, and the *Tao Te Ching*, the text of philosophical Taoism. Regarding human conduct, we can look to what is described in the histories of Tacitus, Thycydides, Polybius, and Diodorus Siculus's *Library of History*. We can look further to the *Moralia* of Plutarch, to the *De rerum natura* of Lucretius, to the *Moral Essays* of Seneca, and to Cicero's *De amicitia (On Friendship)*. In the history of ethics, there is no more complete a guide to the good life than Aristotle's *Ethics*. What we may draw on depends upon the extent of our education.

There is no moral principle that can determine how to act in a given circumstance. The conception of a "categorical imperative" or of the "greatest happiness principle" cannot offer a solution to a particular situation requiring moral choice. Once we realize that ethics is not a science that has a technique for its application implicit within it, we are left with the long-standing practice of prudence. Memory is the source from which we can employ prudence as a guide to moral choice. When we face a circumstance requiring moral choice, we find ourselves in a state of indecision as to our course of action analogous to the state of indecision in the process of reasoning in which conflicting arguments seem equally correct. We experience ignorance.

The ignorance we experience is that taught by Socrates. We know that we do not know. It is an irony that we are human beings but we do not know what it means to be human. We know we are, but we do not know what we are. Satire, as extended irony, is useful as a response to this realization of ignorance. Satire directs our vision of ourselves, reminding us that what *is* is separate from what *ought* to be in human affairs. Satire teaches us to speak freely and to learn to live in the world beside folly. Folly is part of the human; it is never eliminated. Satire teaches us to be human—to have a sense of humor and a sense of the aesthetic.

We may see again the Good, the True, and the Beautiful—the absolutes of Plato and the ancient Greeks. In addition, we may reach the point of the morality of the character of Socrates—to make no one the worse for knowing us and to realize that no harm can come to a good human being, either in life or in death. When we face the distinction between *is* and *ought*, we should know that what can take us from one side of the opposition to the other is the imagination. Through imagination, we can combine judgment with memory. The imagination shows us what might be. It gives a direction to choice, guided by prudence and correct reason.

The freedom of the individual depends not upon a lack of restraint but upon the ability of the individual to be self-determining. Self-determination is accomplished by joining an element of stoicism with an element of cynicism. Neither of these can stand alone successfully. Stoicism, which is at the heart of every speculative sense of philosophy, allows us to accept what we encounter but cannot change, to accept the enduring condition of things. Cynicism offers us the use of humor to modify the stance of stoicism so that the stoic withdrawal into the independence of the self does not become extreme.

Once we combine the ironic humor of cynicism with the independence of stoicism, we find before us both Socrates in the Athenian agora and Epicurus in his Garden, as examples of self-determination and of peace of mind. Then, we can say with the comic playwright, Terence: "I am a human being; I consider nothing human alien to me" (*Homo sum; humani nil a me alienum puto*) (*The Self-Tormentor* 77). Without this sense of the acceptance of life and of self-determination: "We wander ignorant of the peoples and the places" (*Ignari hominumque locorumque erramus*) (Virgil, *Aeneid* 1.332-33).

If we keep the question of self-knowledge before us as we pass through our days, we can hold to the upper road, capable of bearing all evils and all goods, and practice justice with prudence. We shall then, I think, fare well both here and beyond.

Notes

Citations to Greek and Latin literature are to volumes of the Loeb Classical Library of Harvard University Press, with passages occasionally modified in relation to the original and in comparison with other standard translations.

1. Miguel de Cervantes Saavedra, *The Ingenious Hidalgo Don Quixote de la Mancha*, trans. John Rutherford (New York: Penguin, 2003), 12-16.
2. Ibid., 63-64.
3. Desiderius Erasmus, *The Praise of Folly*, trans. Hoyt Hopewell Hudson (Princeton: Princeton University Press, 1974), 37.
4. Ibid., 7.
5. Ibid., 36.
6. Ibid., 8.
7. Ibid., 10.
8. Ibid., 35.
9. Ibid., 28.
10. Ibid., 39.
11. Ibid., 38.
12. Ibid., 43.
13. Ibid., 31.
14. Sebastian Brant, *The Ship of Fools*, trans. Edwin H. Zeydel (New York: Dover, 1962), 363-64. For the original see, Sebastian Brant, *Das Narrenschiff*, 2d ed. Manfred Lemmer (Tübingen: Niemeyer, 1968).
15. Ibid., 58-61.
16. François Rabelais, *Gargantua and Pantagruel*, trans. Burton Raffel (New York: Norton, 1990), 190.
17. Ibid., 191.
18. Ibid.
19. Ibid., 192.
20. Ibid., 195.
21. Ibid.
22. Ibid., 197.
23. John Locke, *An Essay Concerning Human Understanding*, 2 vols., ed. Alexander Campbell Fraser (Oxford: Clarendon, 1894), 1:25.
24. René Descartes, *Discourse on the Method*, in *The Philosophical Writings of Descartes*, 3 vols., trans. John Cottingham, Robert Stoothoff, Dugald Murdoch, and Anthony Kenny (Cambridge: Cambridge University Press, 1994), 1:111.

25. René Descartes, *Discours de la Méthode & Essais*, in vol. 6 of *Oeuvres de Descartes*, ed. Charles Adam and Paul Tannery (Paris: Vrin, 1996), xiii.
26. Jonathan Swift, *The Writings of Jonathan Swift: Authoritative Texts, Backgrounds, Criticism*, ed. Robert A. Greenberg and William Bowman Piper (New York: Norton, 1973). These experiments are described on pp. 152-54.
27. Ibid., 154.
28. Ibid., 153.
29. Ibid., 155.
30. Ibid., 156-57.
31. Ibid., 338.
32. Locke, *Essay*, 1:124.
33. Descartes, *Writings*, 1:20.
34. Locke, *Essay*, 2:146.
35. Descartes, *Writings*, 1:114.
36. Swift, *Writings*, 158-59.
37. G. W. Leibniz, *The Monadology and Other Philosophical Writings*, trans. Robert Latta (Oxford: Oxford University Press, 1951), 247-48; secs. 53-55.
38. Voltaire, *Candide or Optimism*, trans. Theo Cuffe (New York: Penguin, 2005), 110 (Appendix 3). For the French text see, Voltaire, *Dictionnaire philosophique*, ed. Alain Pons (Paris: Gallimard, 1994), 100-106.
39. Ibid., 110.
40. Ibid., 114.
41. Ibid.
42. Ibid., 13.
43. Ibid., 128n3.
44. Ibid.
45. Ibid., 15.
46. Ibid., 88.
47. Ibid., 94.
48. James Joyce, *Finnegans Wake* (London: Faber and Faber, 1939). Interlinear citations are to page and line.
49. Richard Ellmann, *James Joyce*, rev. ed. (New York: Oxford University Press, 1982), 693.
50. Ibid., 703.
51. Jacques Mercanton, "The Hours of James Joyce," in *Portraits of the Artist in Exile: Recollections of James Joyce by Europeans*, ed. Willard Potts (New York: Harcourt, 1986), 229.

52. For Joyce and philosophy, see Donald Phillip Verene, *James Joyce and the Philosophers at "Finnegans Wake"* (Evanston: Northwestern University Press, 2016). For a list of the sixty-five philosophers, see the Appendix: "Register of Philosophers at the Wake."
53. Jorge Luis Borges, *This Craft of Verse*, ed. Calin-Andrei Mihailescu (Cambridge: Harvard University Press, 2000), 88-89.
54. Samuel Beckett, "Dante. . . Bruno. Vico. . Joyce," in *Our Exagmination Round His Factification for Incamination of Work in Progress* (New York: New Directions, 1939), 15-16.
55. James Joyce, *A Portrait of the Artist as a Young Man* (New York: Penguin, 1976), 275-76.
56. Johann Wolfgang von Goethe, *Zur Farbenlehre*, in *Goethes Sämtliche Werke*. Jubiläums-Ausgabe, vol. 40 (Stuttgart and Berlin: J.G. Cotta'sche Buchhandlung, n.d.), 154. My trans.
57. Pierre Hadot, *What is Ancient Philosophy?*, trans. Michael Chase (Cambridge: Harvard University Press, 2002), 30. See *Theaetetus* 149a.
58. Goethe, *Zur Farbenlehre*, 154-55. My trans.
59. Anton-Hermann Chroust, *Aristotle: Protrepticus, A Reconstruction* (Notre Dame, IN: University of Notre Dame Press, 1964), 9-10.
60. Lina Bolzoni, *Il teatro della memoria. Studi su Giulio Camillo* (Padua: Liviana, 1984), xiii.
61. *L'idea del theatro dell'eccellen M. Giulio Camillo* (Florence: Lorenzo Torrentino, 1550), 7. My trans.
62. Lu Beery Wenneker, "An Examination of *L'idea del theatro* of Giulio Camillo, Including an Annotated Translation, with Special Attention to His Influence on Emblem Literature and Iconography." Ph.D. Dissertation, University of Pittsburgh, 1970.
63. Frances A. Yates, *The Art of Memory* (Chicago: University of Chicago Press, 1966), chaps. 6 and 7.
64. *L'idea del theatro*, 7. My trans.
65. *Hermetica*, trans. Brian P. Copenhaver (Cambridge: Cambridge University Press, 1992), 67.
66. Marsilio Ficino, *Commentaries on Plato*, vol. 2, *Parmenides, Part 1*, ed. and trans. Maude Vanhaelen (Cambridge: Harvard University Press, 2012), 3.
67. Giovanni Pico della Mirandola, "Oration on the Dignity of Man," trans. Elizabeth Livermore Forbes, in *The Renaissance Philosophy of Man*, ed. Ernst Cassirer, Paul Oskar Kristeller, and John Herman Randall, Jr. (Chicago: University of Chicago Press, 1948), 229.
68. Yates, *Art of Memory*, 141.
69. Ibid., 147-48.
70. Giambattista Vico, *The Autobiography of Giambattista Vico*, trans. Max Harold Fisch and Thomas Goddard Bergin (Ithaca: Cornell University Press, 1990), 199-200.

71. Karl-Otto Apel, *Die Idee der Sprache in der Tradition des Humanismus von Dante bis Vico*, 2d ed. (Bonn: Bouvier Verlag Herbert Grundmann, 1975), 320-21; G. W. F. Hegel, *Grundlinien der Philosophie des Rechts* (Hamburg: Meiner, 1955), 17.

72. Giambattista Vico, *The New Science of Giambattista Vico*, trans. Thomas Goddard Bergin and Max Harold Fisch (Ithaca: Cornell University Press, 1984). Italian edition: Giambattista Vico, *Opere*, 2 vols., ed. Andrea Battistini (Milan: Mondadori, 1990). Interlinear citations are to the paragraph numbers common to all English translations and most Italian editions. See also, Donald Phillip Verene, *Vico's "New Science": A Philosophical Commentary* (Ithaca: Cornell University Press, 2015).

73. James Joyce, *Ulysses*, ed. Hans Walter Gabler (New York: Random House, 1986), 28.

74. Vico, *Autobiography*, 182. See also, Donald Phillip Verene, *The New Art of Autobiography: An Essay on the "Life of Giambattista Vico Written by Himself"* (Oxford: Clarendon, 1991).

75. G. W. F. Hegel, *Phänomenologie des Geistes*, ed. Johannes Hoffmeister (Hamburg: Meiner, 6th ed., 1952); English trans., *The Phenomenology of Spirit*, trans. Michael Inwood (Oxford: Oxford University Press, 2018). Interlinear citations are to the paragraph enumeration in this and other translations, such as those by Miller and Pinkard. Citations to the Hoffmeister German edition are to page numbers.

76. *Briefe von und an Hegel*, ed. Johannes Hoffmeister, 4 vols. (Hamburg: Meiner, 1952-60), 1:99-100. My trans.

77. Ernst Cassirer, *The Philosophy of Symbolic Forms*, Vol. 2, *Mythical Thought* (New Haven: Yale University Press, 1955), xvi. On Cassirer's philosophy of myth, see Donald Phillip Verene, *The Origins of the Philosophy of Symbolic Forms: Kant, Hegel, and Cassirer* (Evanston: Northwestern University Press, 2011), chap. 2.

78. Ernst Bloch, "Zerstörte Sprache—zerstörte Kultur," in *Deutsche Literatur in Exil 1933-1945: Texte und Dokumente*, ed. Michael Winkler (Stuttgart: Reclam, 1979), 353-54. My trans.

79. See Donald Phillip Verene, *Hegel's Recollection: A Study of Images in the "Phenomenology of Spirit"* (Albany: State University of New York Press, 1985), 36. Hegel's fragment is called "Über Mythologie, Volkgeist und Kunst." See Eva Ziesche, "Unbekannte Manuskripte aus der Jenaer und Nürnberger Zeit im Berliner Hegel-Nachlass," *Zeitschrift für philosphische Forschung* 29 (1975): 430-44.

80. G. W. F. Hegel, *The Science of Logic*, trans. George di Giovanni (Cambridge: Cambridge University Press, 2010), 29.

81. Dante Alighieri, *The Divine Comedy*, trans. John Ciardi (New York: New American Library, 2003). For the Italian and English opposed text, see *The Divine Comedy*, 3 vols., trans. with commentary by Charles S. Singleton (Princeton: Princeton University Press, 1970, 1973, and 1977). On Joyce and Dante, see Mary T. Reynolds, *Joyce and Dante: The Shaping Imagination* (Princeton: Princeton University Press, 1981), esp. "Appendix: Joyce's Allusions to Dante."
82. Archibald MacLeish, "Ars Poetica," in *The Oxford Book of American Poetry*, ed. David Lehman (New York: Oxford, 2006), 385-86.
83. Joyce, *Ulysses*, 20.
84. Mercanton, "The Hours of James Joyce," 221.
85. A. N. Whitehead, *Modes of Thought* (New York: Capricorn, 1958), 238.
86. Francesco Guicciardini, *Ricordi* (Milan: Rizzoli, 1977), 131. My trans.

Index

Anaxagoras, 44, 77, 104
Anselm, Saint, 43
Apel, Karl-Otto, 91
Aquinas, Thomas, Saint, 60
Arcesilaus, 35
Aristophanes, 13, 18, 27-30, 104
Aristotle, 13, 16, 34, 37, 60-61, 79-83
   ethics, 16, 34, 38, 81-82, 110
   on metaphor, 16, 95
   on poetics, 68
   on topics, 21, 42
Augustine, Saint, 56, 60
Bacon, Francis, 60
Bayle, Pierre, 50
Beckett, Samuel, 61
Blake, William, 106
Bloch, Ernst, 100
Bolzoni, Lina, 85
Borges, Jorge Luis, 61
Brant, Sebastian, 40
Camillo, Giulio, 13, 85-89
Carneades, 35
Cassirer, Ernst, 98
Cervantes, Miguel de, Saavedra, 17-18
Cicero, 10, 19, 37, 88-89, 110
Claudius, 17
D'Alembert, Jean Le Rond, 47
Dante, 60, 91, 93, 103-5, 109
Democritus, 33
Descartes, René, 47-48, 51, 60
Diderot, Denis, 47
Diodorus Siculus, 110
Diogenes Laertius, 27, 76
Diogenes of Sinope, 32

Duns Scotus, 43
Epicurus, 17, 34, 56-57, 111
Erasmus, Desiderius, 13, 18, 28, 35, 37-40
Ficino, Marsilio, 86
Goethe, Johann Wolfgang von, 60, 73, 79, 109
Guicciardini, Francesco, 109
Hadot, Pierre, 76
Hammurabi, 109
Hegel, Georg William Friedrich, 10, 13, 60, 91, 97-102, 106
Heraclitus, 33
Hesiod, 13, 67-71, 74, 105-6
Homer, 60, 67, 70, 92, 97, 106, 109
Horace, 15-17
Joyce, James, 13, 18, 35, 59-63, 92, 103-7
Juvenal, 17
Kant, Immanuel, 60, 97
Kristensen, Tom, 59
Leibniz, Georg Wilhelm, 53-56, 87
Leon, tyrant of Phlius, 15
Lindemann, Ferdinand von, 104
Locke, John, 47-48, 51
Lucian, 18, 31-35, 37
Lucilius, 16
Lucretius, 67, 110
Luther, Martin, 97
MacLeish, Archibald, 106
Mercanton, Jacques, 59
Mettrie, Julien Offray de la, 47
More, Thomas, 37
Muses, 11, 71, 74, 94, 96, 101, 105-6, 109
   description of, 67-68
   and myth of cicadas, 73-74

Nicholas of Cusa, 60
Nero, 17
Noah, 93
Petronius, 17
Pico della Mirandola, 42, 87
Plato, 9, 15, 17, 27, 60, 67, 73-78, 106
  absolutes, 110
  as Academic philosopher, 31, 33
  on doctrine of Forms, 30
  warning on his teaching, 86
Platus, 43
Plutarch, 110
Polybius, 110
Pyrrho of Elis, 34-35
Pythagoras, 15, 31-32, 42, 76
Quintilian, 20, 37
Rabelais, François, 13, 18, 28, 35, 41-45, 54
Schiller, Johann Christoph Friedrich, 101, 106
Seneca, 110
Seven Sages, 9
Shakespeare, William, 17, 37, 60, 109
Simonides, 19-21
Socrates, 31, 39, 74-78, 91, 110
  Aristophanes's attack on, 13, 18, 27-30
  on death, 15
  on ignorance, 11, 35, 38-40, 42
  on Platonic Forms, 30
  on poetry, 60
  on self-knowledge, 9-12, 23, 76-77
  on use of language, 43, 97
Solomon, 44
Stevenson, Robert Louis Balfour, 61
Swift, Jonathan, 13, 18, 28, 35, 47-52
Tacitus, 110
Tasso, Torquato, 95
Thales, 9, 76
Thycydides, 110
Terence, 43, 111
Vaucanson, Jacques de, 47
Vico, Giambattista, 13, 60, 91-96, 105-6
Virgil, 106, 111
Vitruvius, 88
Voltaire, François Marie Arouet, 13, 18, 28, 35, 53-57
Voss, Johann Heinrich, 97
Whitehead, Alfred North, 106
William of Ockham, 43
Xenophon, 76
Yates, Frances, 85, 87